Rogues, Writers & Whores:
Dining with the Rich and Infamous

Even today it is not common knowledge that the Marquis de Sade's appetite for fine food was almost as intense as his appetite for rape and sodomy. Even when in prison, he dined well—in the Bastille, for example, he whiled away five years drinking fine Claret and eating truffled oysters.

Daniel Rogov

Rogues, &Writers &Whores

Dining with the Rich & Infamous

ILLUSTRATED BY

Yael Hershberg

The Toby Press

Rogues, Writers & Whores: Dining with the Rich and Infamous
First Edition, 2007

The Toby Press LLC
POB 8531, New Milford, CT 06676-8531, USA
& POB 2455, London W1A 5WY, England

www.tobypress.com

ISBN: 978 1 59264 172 7

A CIP catalogue record for this title
is available from the British Library

Printed and bound in the United States

For Rachel
Without her contribution this
book would not have been.

Contents

viii

x

xi

Introduction

The beginning and root of all good is to make the stomach happy; wisdom and learning are founded on that.　　　—Epicurus

Happy and successful cooking doesn't rely only on know-how; it comes from the heart, makes great demands on the palate, and needs enthusiasm and a great love of food to bring it to life.　　　—Georges Blanc

I hate people who are not serious about their meals.　　　—Oscar Wilde

To reflect on gastronomy is to call to mind great chefs who have dedicated their lives to the preparation of fine food and the creation of new dishes; it is also to think of the kings and courtesans for whom culinary inventions have been named and of those restaurants that serve meals so superb that their names are embedded forever in our memory. However, when it comes to thinking about great food, most people give little or no credit to the gourmet.

It is true that without great chefs there would be no great dishes, but one has to bear in mind that such dedication to the preparation of fine food demands to be matched by equal dedication to its consumption and appreciation. This is the role of gourmets, a distinct species of people who give priority in all human affairs to the discriminate pleasures of the palate.

To the gourmet, this connoisseur of fine food and drink, gastronomy is part of a humanistic vision. After all, one of the reasons we human beings are unique is because we are the only animals who cook our food, and are capable of eating when we are not hungry. Nothing could be more gratifying to the gourmet than the satisfaction of the palate, and no social act is more enjoyable than that of sharing a meal and meditating on its merits. Literary critic Charles Augustin Sainte-Beuve, a famous gourmet in nineteenth century France, bemoaned the fact that he had to earn a living in the following words: "But rejoice my little stomach, for all that I earn is yours."

Perhaps the best description of the culinary art is given by the great nineteenth century chef, Antonin Carême: "Dining has much in common with painting and music. The painter, by richness of colors, produces works that seduce the eye and the imagination; the musician, by the combination of his notes, produces harmony and the sense of hearing receives the sweetest sensations that melody can produce. Our culinary combinations are of the same nature. The gourmet's palate and sense of smell receive sensations similar to those of the connoisseurs of painting and music."

What Carême neglected to mention is that the culinary art is the most selfless of all art-forms, because it is, by definition, perishable. What the sculptor Jean Tinguely accomplished with his self-destroying machines is achieved by every great chef every time one of his dishes is brought to the table. Its function is to be consumed. The only traces of the dish that are left are in the mind of the person who experienced its rich tastes and aromas, and the best one to testify to its worth is the gourmet, who often records his impressions, thus codifying and canonizing the cuisine of his time.

There are those who would denigrate the importance of gastronomy as a driving force in human life, but such people are, at least in the eyes of gourmets, simply uninformed. Anthropologists and sociologists concur, for example, that gastronomy ranks with all of the other social sciences as a means of defining the culture of a nation or a community. In fact, starting from the second half of the twentieth century, the anthropology of food became an independent discipline dedicated to exploring the production, distribution and preparation of food in relation to economic systems, labor divisions, gender roles and class relationship. A wedding cake, a Christmas dinner, or utensils found in a Roman excavation all signify forces interacting in a society in a given time. Semiologist Roland Barthes observed that food "is a system of communication, a body of images, a protocol of usages, situations and behavior."

One can presume that a team of anthropologists examining the buried remains of a French city twenty centuries from now for example, might well conclude that theirs was a society which applied as much method and energy to eating as to thinking. They would find that during the last decade of the twentieth century, four out of every ten shops in Paris, and as many as fifty percent of all the industries in France, were devoted to filling stomachs.

Even in the study of history, gastronomy plays a critical role, and a history of the world could be written from the (albeit admittedly limited) viewpoint of the intestinal tract. Such a history would record, for example, that at least one person sold his birthright for a "mess of pottage." It would also point out that after Napoleon conquered Egypt he dined on a garlic stew and then suffered an upset stomach. Thinking he had been poisoned, he decided to return to France and called off his plan to conquer Jerusalem.

It is true that gourmets tend to exaggerate a bit. To the true gourmet, art means Watteau's *Embarquement pour Cythère*, which portrays eighteenth century courtiers picnicking, and Manet's *Déjeuner sur l'Herbe*, in which one nude and another flimsily dressed woman picnic with two fully-clothed men. Literature is James Joyce's short story, "The Dead," the entire tale taking place around a sumptuously set table; Anatole France's description of the restaurant in Paris' Rue Vavin, where the only dish was cassoulet; and Ernest Hemingway's lunch at Brasserie Lipp in *A Moveable Feast*. The wedding meal in *Madame Bovary*, on the other hand, is largely ignored, as discriminating diners have never fully forgiven Flaubert for writing, in his *L'Education Sentimentale*, that "bottles of wine were left to heat on the stove." Gourmets have a special place in their hearts for Chateaubriand, not so much for his poetry and diaries, but because when he visited Dante's grave in Florence he plucked several laurel leaves which he carefully put into his pocket, for "there is nothing better with macaroni."

Food has been a favorite literary topic since the time of Epicurus. If Homer is to be believed, Odysseus spent as much time in feasting as he did in warfare; the characters in Chaucer's *Canterbury Tales* devote as much time to dining as they did to fornicating; and Rabelais' Gargantua would have been little more than an oversized oaf, had it not been for his magnificent dining habits. However, the greatest impact of the culinary arts on literature was during the nineteenth century.

Starting in the 1850s, the question of cuisine became a major subject matter in the writings of men and women of letters. Authors were particularly fond of writing about the pleasures of the dinner table, and many pages in novels were devoted to detailed descriptions of culinary feasts. Charles Lamb devoted an entire essay to the joy of eating roast pork, "Pig: Let Me Speak his Praise"; William Thackeray wrote a poem of praise named *The Ballad of Bouillabaisse*, and Herman Melville, describing a whale dinner, wrote that "when you come to sit down before a meat-pie nearly thirty-three meters long, it tends to take away your appetite."

Throughout history, a collection of famous and infamous men and women have contributed, in their sometimes perverted but almost always intriguing ways, to the world of gastronomy. The stories of those people, their culinary habits and the dishes either created by them, named after them or cherished by them are the subject of this book. Kings and queens, dukes and duchesses, chefs and restaurateurs, novelists and composers—rogues, writers and whores—all have had dishes named after them. Some generals are remembered more for the luxurious meals they served than for their military successes, and at least a handful of courtesans have entered the history books because of the dishes they either invented or had named after them.

Since, as Voltaire reminds us, there is no history but only fictions of varying degrees of plausibility, our knowledge of the past is invariably constructed on a mixture of facts and fictions. Therefore, most of what we 'know' about the dining habits of famous people is based as much on myth as it is on fact. Fully separating out the myths from the realities would be impossible, and, in any case, would serve no purpose but to deprive us of a great deal of pleasure.

Several Notes about the Recipes

Readers will notice that some of the recipes are simple and require only basic experience in the kitchen, while others are time-consuming and difficult to prepare. Although even the most complex of the recipes can be executed by a diligent cook, a gourmet knows one can extract as much pleasure from the reading of such a recipe as one could in dining upon the dish.

In the spirit of the chefs who devised these recipes, only the freshest and highest quality ingredients should be used. As not one of these chefs would have dreamed of using tinned or frozen foods, powdered soup mixes or substitutes, neither should the readers about to execute the recipes in their kitchen.

When oven temperatures are given, it is assumed that all ovens have been preheated and oven temperatures in both Fahrenheit and Celsius will be found on page 325.

Feast of the Gods

T he life of Lucius Licinius Lucullus Ponticus, perhaps the most famous epicure of all time, was described by Plutarch as an ancient comedy that begins with political and military campaigns, and ends with drinking bouts and outrageous banquets. Plutarch disapproved of Lucullus' extravagant living, which included costly villas, magnificent gardens and a huge collection of paintings and statues. However, to his compatriots, this Roman general and consul who campaigned successfully in Asia Minor and returned with a fortune had become a hero.

In celebration of his triumph over the Mithridates and the Tigranes, Lucullus gave the senate a banquet on the Capitol and arranged a public feast for the common people in which one hundred thousand jars of Greek wine were distributed. According to Pliny the elder, when Lucullus attended public functions he was accompanied by a slave who had the special task of seeing that his master did not eat too much.

His dinners became the highlight of Roman life, and notables such as Cato, Cicero, Crassus and Pompey all vied for invitations to those luxurious events. His guests drank from beakers set with precious stones and were entertained with choruses and recitations as they dined on a variety of meats. Plutarch called him "the envy of the vulgar" but also noted that Lucullus was the liberal patron of Greek philosophers and had a vast library.

Whether he was entertaining senators and consuls or dining alone, Lucullus served only the best of foods and spared no effort or expense in obtaining them. Smoked meats were imported from Gaul, pickles from Spain, wines from the Jurasian Alps, pomegranates from Libya, oysters from Britain, and spices from the Far East. Lucullus is also said to have been the first to bring sweet cherries and apricots to Rome.

On one occasion, Cicero and Pompey met Lucullus in the Forum and challenged him to prepare a dinner that same day. They refused to allow him to discuss the arrangements with his servants except to tell them the location of the event. But it was with this very piece of information that Lucullus outwitted his guests, as every room in each of his villas had its own pre-established budget and thus by instructing them to hold the dinner in the Apollo room, the servants knew in what style it was to be served. The expense spent on the Apollo dinner was fifty thousand drachmas, but in fact, Cicero and Pompey were more amazed by the rapidity of the outlay than by the luxury.

Once, when dining alone at home, Lucullus was shocked when his servants presented him with a simple supper of eggs and porridge, demanding of them "What, were you not informed that today Lucullus was dining with Lucullus? Where is the feast befitting the honor and station of my most esteemed of guests?"

The feasts at Lucullus' estates became a major source of sustenance for many Roman notables, so much so that upon his death it was said that half of Rome suffered from indigestion.

Langue de veau Lucullus
Veal Tongue Lucullus

1 lb (450 gr) cooked veal tongue, at room temperature	1 Tbsp olive oil
	3–4 cloves garlic, sliced
	salt and pepper to taste
½ lb (225 gr) goose liver	*demi-glace* or Espagnole sauce
4 Tbsp butter	for serving (see p. 94)

Slice the veal tongue about ¼″ (½ cm) thick and cut the goose liver into 8 equal slices.

In a heavy skillet heat 2 Tbsp of the butter together with the olive oil and in this heat the tongue slices just until they begin to brown. With a spatula remove the slices and set aside to keep warm. Add the remaining butter, heat through and in this sauté the goose liver slices until nicely browned on the exterior but still pink inside. Season with salt and pepper to taste and set aside to keep warm.

Heat the *demi-glace* or Espagnole sauce through. To serve place a slice of goose liver on each of the tongue slices and then spoon over the sauce. Serve immediately. (Serves 4 as a main course or 8 as a first course).

Spiced Beef Lucullus

1 beef brisket, about 11 lb (5 kilos), weighed with the bone	6 Tbsp honey
	2 small onions, unpeeled and halved
1½ Tbsp whole black peppercorns	4 medium carrots, halved lengthwise
1½ tsp whole cloves	2 stalks celery, halved
5 Tbsp coarse salt	¼ cup celery leaves
3 bay leaves, crumbled	

Have the butcher remove the bone and excess fat from the beef brisket.

In a small bowl crush the peppercorns and cloves together. Add the salt, bay leaves and honey. Mix well. Lay the meat on a large earthenware dish and rub it on all sides with the honey mixture. Cover the dish with greaseproof paper and let stand 3 days, refrigerated, turning and rubbing with the marinade twice daily.

Just before cooking, wash the meat under cold running water and pat dry with toweling. Roll the meat and tie with kitchen string. Transfer the tied meat roll to a flameproof casserole dish, and add the onions, carrots, celery, celery leaves and water just to cover. Bring to a boil, cover and let simmer for 2 hours.

Remove the meat from the casserole dish and set aside to cool. When thoroughly cool, cover and refrigerate overnight. Serve cold the following day. (Serves 8–10).

Marcus Gavius Apicius, born c. 25 BCE
Patron of Good Fare

W hen Marcus Gavius Apicius realized that his fortune had shrunk to a mere ten million sesterces, about five hundred thousand dollars in today's terms, he feared he could no longer dine in the style to which he was accustomed. Facing such a calamity, he decided to end his life by poisoning himself during a banquet arranged especially for that purpose. This famous Roman epicure, who was born around 25 BCE and lived during the reign of Tiberius, was famous for his extravagant entertaining. He invented numerous new dishes and some claim that he is the author of the oldest collection of recipes still in existence, *De re coquinaria* (*On Cookery*). It is also believed that he founded the School for Good Fare referred to by Seneca.

Apicius is known to have spent huge sums of money on exotic ingredients such as camels' hooves and nightingales' tongues in order to please the many distinguished guests, including Emperor Tiberius, who frequented his palatial villa in Minturno, not far from Naples. Once, he sailed to Libya in search of giant shrimps but returned empty handed after tasting the poor offerings of the local fishermen. According to Pliny, Apicius fed his pigs with dried figs and gorged them to death with overdoses of honeyed wine. Some believe he also had his

geese force fed with figs in order to enlarge their livers, and thus was, perhaps, the originator of *foie gras*.

Among his quirks, Apicius sometimes planned his menus to suit the sign of the zodiac of his most honored guest. For those born under the sign of Libra, for example, he would serve what he considered "a balanced diet" that combined sweet, sour and spicy, using gentle spices such as saffron and rosemary. For those born under the sign of Scorpio he would prepare heavier, highly spiced stews, and for honored guests born under Pisces he would present a menu in which as many as fourteen different fish courses might be served.

As to the origin of *De re coquinaria*, a valuable text that allows us an insight into the diet of the Romans, some historians suspect that the book was not authored by Gavius Apicius at all, but by Caelius Apicius of the third or fourth century CE, who is thought to have used the suffix Apicius in order to link the work with the culinary fame of his predecessor. Others speculate that his name, *Caelii Apicius*, i.e. the Apicius of Caelius, suggests that author was in fact Greek and not Roman. Still, most historians agree that the compilation is largely based on the recipes of Gavius Apicius, with additional recipes from ancient times.

The ten books include almost five hundred recipes for meats, vegetables, legumes, fowl, meat, seafood, and fish, and many recipes feature *garum*, a fermented fish sauce that was a common staple in ancient Rome. Relying heavily on vinegar, possibly to hide the smell of spoiled meat, very few of the dishes so adored by Apicius would be considered tasty today. The following recipes, therefore, are inventions of modern chefs who have named many dishes in honor of Apicius over the years.

Potage Apicius

2 cups chicken stock
1 chicken breast, boned
½ cup + 2 tsp butter
1¼ lb (565 gr) smoked beef
   tongue, in thin slices
½ cup mushrooms, chopped
   coarsely
1¼ lb lasagna noodles

12 cups chicken consommé
½ tsp freshly ground black
   pepper
pinch of nutmeg
¾ cup Parmesan cheese, grated
¼ tsp lemon juice
salt as required

In a saucepan bring the chicken stock to a boil and in this cook the chicken breast until thoroughly cooked. Drain the breast and puree the meat finely.

In a skillet melt 2 tsp of the butter and in this sauté the mushrooms lightly. With a slotted spoon remove the mushrooms and set aside to keep warm. In the same skillet, lightly sauté the tongue slices, adding butter only if the skillet becomes dry. Set the tongue slices aside to keep warm.

In a large saucepan bring a large amount of lightly salted water to the boil and into this plunge the lasagna noodles. Drain the noodles immediately and rinse them under cold running water.

In a separate saucepan bring the consommé to the boil and boil until reduced by nearly half. When the consommé is reduced, add the remaining butter, the pepper and the nutmeg and in this simmer the lasagna noodles for 20 minutes. Remove from the flame. With a slotted spoon transfer the lasagna noodles to a large mixing bowl. Cover the consommé and let stand until ready for further use. Add the pureed chicken breast to the noodles and mix well with a wooden spoon.

In a soup tureen place 1 layer of the lasagna noodles and on this distribute a layer of tongue slices. Over these spread the mushrooms and sprinkle with Parmesan cheese. Continue to build layers until the noodles, tongue and cheese are all used. Pour over the consommé and serve immediately. (Serves 8).

Kidneys Apicius

4 veal kidneys, with some of the fat left intact, sliced thinly
2¼ cups chicken consommé
1 cup rice
6 Tbsp butter
2 shallots, chopped finely

¼ cup Madeira or Port wine
1 cup brown sauce, e.g. *demi-glace*, Espagnole (see p. 94)
salt and freshly ground pepper to taste
¼ cup pine nuts
¼ tsp ground coriander

In a saucepan bring the consommé to a boil and in this cook the rice until it is done. Set aside to keep warm.

In a large heavy skillet melt 3 Tbsp of the butter and in this sauté the shallots for 1 minute. Add the kidney slices and sauté over a high flame just until the red color disappears. Add the Madeira and simmer briskly for about 2 minutes. Remove the kidney slices and set aside to keep warm. Reduce the flame, add the brown sauce and season to taste with salt and pepper. Heat through without boiling again.

Mix the remaining butter together with the rice. Add the pine nuts, coriander and salt and pepper to taste and toss well. To serve, mound the rice in the center of a preheated serving dish and surround with the kidney slices. Spoon over the brown sauce. (Serves 4–6).

Roast Quail Apicius

8 quails, trussed
3 Tbsp olive oil
1–2 Tbsp dried thyme
6 dates, pitted and chopped
2 Tbsp onion, chopped
2 cloves garlic, crushed

1 anchovy fillet, chopped
1 cup dry white wine
1 Tbsp honey
1 Tbsp white wine vinegar
1 egg yolk
white pepper to taste

Brush the quails with about 1 Tbsp of the olive oil, sprinkle over the dried thyme and bake in a medium oven until the birds are done (about 25–30 minutes).

Combine the dates, onion, garlic, anchovy fillet and the remaining olive oil and work to a fine paste with a mortar and pestle or a food processor and then slowly add the remaining ingredients, processing until the mixture is smooth throughout. Serve hot by spooning part of the sauce over the birds and serving the remaining sauce separately. (Serves 4).

Taillevent, 1310–1395

The Founding Father

Little is known about Guillaume Tirel, most commonly known as Taillevent, a fourteenth century cook who wrote what is considered to be the founding text of French gastronomy; a valuable medieval collection of recipes recording the cuisine of a royal household. Other than the Roman *De re coquinaria* by Apicius, there were hardly any written recipes until Taillevent compiled *Le Viandier de Taillevent*, the full title of which reads as follows: "Hereafter follows the *Viandier* describing the preparation of all manner of foods, as cooked by Taillevent, the cook of our noble king, and also the dressing and preparation of boiled meat, roasts, sea and freshwater fish, sauces, spices, and other suitable and necessary things as described hereafter."

Taillevent started his career as a kitchen boy in the kitchen of Jeanne d'Evreux, Queen of France, where he probably got his lifelong nickname, which means wind-slicer and is attributed to his prominent nose. In 1346 he became a cook for King Philip VI, and in later years he went on to serve as *première écuyer de cuisine*, chief cook, for Kings Charles V and Charles VI. In 1388 Charles VI promoted him to be the master of the kitchen stores. *Le Viandier de Taillevent* was probably written for Charles V between 1373 and 1380, with a second, longer version, written in the late 1380s under Charles VI. Taillevent died in 1395 and almost a century passed before the book appeared in print, shortly after printing was introduced in the 1450s. Fifteen editions were published between 1490 and 1604, of which only five copies survived to the twentieth century.

It is believed today that *Le Viandier*, which includes over two hundred recipes, is partly a compilation of older recipes from the late thirteenth and early fourteenth centuries. Taillevent was the most famous chef of his time and his book inspired other culinary works, among them *Le Mésnagier de Paris*, written in 1393 by a wealthy Parisian for his fifteen-year-old bride, and the 1420 *Du Fait de Cuisine* by Chiquart Amiczo, chef to the Duke of Savoy.

In Taillevent's day, Paris benefited from a vast array of foods: a choice of fifty different varieties of sea and fresh-water fish, a multitude of home grown vegetables and various ingredient and spices such as sugar, buckwheat, aniseed, cinnamon, ginger, nutmeg, pepper and saffron, brought to France by the Crusaders. Taillevent's recipes rely heavily on the use of spices. Some believe this was done in order to camouflage the smells and flavors of meats and fish that had spoiled due to lack of proper storage, but others argue that the precious spices were used so lavishly in order to flaunt social distinction.

Nearly all of Taillevent's recipes were written in a short, abbreviated, almost crude manner, giving few details on the amount of ingredients to be used, and taking a great deal of interpretation by those trying to replicate them.

Tortes de harbe, fromaige, et œuf
Herb and Cheese Torte—
Taillevent's Recipe

Take parsley, mint, chard, spinach, lettuce, marjoram, basil and wild thyme, and grind everything together in a mortar, moisten with pure water and squeeze out the juice; break a large number of eggs into the juice and add powdered ginger, cinnamon and long pepper, a good quality cheese, grated, and salt; beat everything together. Then make a very thin pastry to put in your dish, of the size of your dish, and then line your dish with it; coat the inside of the dish with pork fat, then put in your pastry, put your dish on the coals and again coat the inside of the pastry with pork fat; when it has melted, put your filling in your pastry and cover it with the other dish and put fire on top as well as underneath and let your pie dry out a little; uncover the top of the dish and put five egg yolks and fine spice powder carefully over your pie; then replace the dish as it was before and let it gradually cook in a low coal fire; check often to see that it is not overcooking. Put sugar over the top when serving it.

Torte aux herbes, fromage et œufs
Herb and Cheese Torte—
The Modern Adaptation

pastry dough for 9″ (23 cm) pie crust

bacon slices or pork fat for lining pie dish

½ cup fresh parsley, chopped

1 Tbsp mint, chopped

¼ lb (115 gr) each spinach, romaine lettuce and Swiss chard, chopped

5 egg yolks

1 Tbsp fresh marjoram, chopped finely

1 Tbsp fresh basil, chopped finely

1 tsp fresh thyme, chopped finely

1 Tbsp sugar

½ tsp ginger

½ tsp cinnamon

¼ tsp black pepper

6 oz cheddar cheese, grated

6 oz mozzarella cheese, cut into small cubes

½ tsp salt

Line a pie tin with the bacon slices or pork fat and on this place the dough for the pie crust. Fill the pie tin with uncooked rice and bake in an oven that has been pre-heated to hot for about 10 minutes. Remove from the oven and set the rice aside for use in other dishes. Reset the oven temperature to medium.

In a mixing bowl combine the parsley, mint, spinach, lettuce and chard. Add the egg yolks, marjoram, basil and thyme and mix well. Transfer this mixture to the pie crust and bake until the mixture is set (about 20 minutes).

While the pie is baking mix together the remaining ingredients in a bowl. After the mixture in the pie shell has set remove the pie from the oven, spread these ingredients on the pie, sprinkle lightly with water and return to the oven until the pie is firm (about 20 minutes longer). Remove from the oven and let cool for 4–5 minutes. Cover the pie with a pre-warmed serving plate and quickly turn the pie so that it falls out of its case. Discard the bacon and serve the pie hot or at room temperature. (Serves 4–6).

Tarte au champignons
Mushroom Tarte

¾ lb (350 gr) Champignon
    mushrooms, cleaned and
    trimmed
¼ lb (225 gr) Porcini
    mushrooms, well cleaned
¼ lb (225 gr) grated cheddar
    cheese
2 Tbsp olive oil

½ tsp salt
freshly ground black pepper to
    taste
¼ tsp dry mustard powder
1 clove garlic, crushed
butter as required
pastry dough for 1 covered 9″
    (23 cm) pie crust

In a small saucepan bring lightly salted water to the boil and into this plunge the champignon and porcini mushrooms for 30 seconds. Drain the mushrooms, pat dry with paper toweling and slice them thinly. To the mushrooms add the olive oil, cheese, salt, pepper, mustard powder and garlic. Mix well, cover and refrigerate overnight.

    Butter the pie tin and line with the pastry dough, piercing the bottom several times with the tines of a fork. Fill the pie tin with the cheese and mushroom mixture until nearly full and top with the remaining pastry dough, piercing the top twice with the tines of a fork. Transfer the pie to an oven that has been preheated to hot until the top crust is golden brown (15–18 minutes). Let cool for 10 minutes and serve hot. (Serves 4–6).

Gâteau Taillevent
Taillevent Cake

FOR THE CAKE:
1 cup almonds
⅔ cup butter
⅔ cup sugar
5 eggs, separated
grated rind of one orange

⅔ cup ricotta cheese
6 Tbsp flour
candied fruits for garnish

FOR THE GLAZE:

4 Tbsp apricot jam   2 Tbsp brandy

Place the almonds in a dry skillet and roast them slowly over a medium heat. Slice the almonds and set aside.

Cream the butter together with ½ cup of the sugar and then add the egg yolks. Mix thoroughly and then add the grated orange rind, ricotta and flour.

In a separate bowl whip the egg whites until stiff and into those beat in the remaining sugar.

Gently fold the egg white mixture into the dough and transfer this batter to a well-buttered 9″ springform pan. Bake in an oven that has been preheated to medium-hot until the center of the cake is set (about 30 minutes). Remove from the oven, let the cake cool in the pan, run a sharp knife around the outside edge and then release to a serving plate.

Prepare the glaze: In a small saucepan heat the jam together with 1 Tbsp of water, stirring constantly until a simmer is obtained, and the jam takes on a liquid nature. Press the jam through a sieve into a small bowl and stir in the brandy. Pour this glaze evenly over the cake as it is cooling. Garnish with candied fruits. (Serves 6).

Agnès Sorel, 1421–1450

Muse of Chefs

From time to time, and in every age, whores have directed the affairs of kings," remarked Catherine de Medici, who endured a bitter rivalry with Diane de Poitiers, the mistress of her husband, King Henri II.

A hundred years earlier, Marie d'Anjou, Queen of France and wife of King Charles VII, would have probably agreed with de Medici, as she had a similar rivalry with her husband's mistress, Agnès Sorel, the first official royal mistress in French history. Sorel met the king when she was twenty, while serving as a lady-in-waiting to Isabelle de Lorraine, wife of the king's brother-in-law René d'Anjou. She joined the French court in Chinon in 1444, and Charles, who was utterly devoted to her, gave her the Château de Loches in the Loire Valley, bestowed upon her precious jewelry and granted her status equal to that of a princess. He also legitimized the three daughters she bore him.

Witty and opinionated as well as beautiful, Sorel was a woman with an enormous ego, and as the king's mistress she was not content to merely bask in the reflected glory of the throne or to have her dress bills paid; she also exerted great social and political influence. Her influence in world affairs was probably most felt when she persuaded Charles to oust the British from France. According to the Abbot of Brantome,

a sixteenth century chronicler of social mores, it was on "the unique advice of his mistress that the king left his gardens and hunts and took the bit between the teeth, thus making his way off to the catastrophic war that followed."

While carrying their fourth child, at age twenty-eight, Sorel joined the king on campaign against the English in Jumièges, Normandy. There she suddenly fell ill and, according to official accounts, died of "stomach flux". However, many believed that she was poisoned by her enemies, and a recent finding of abnormal levels of mercury in her remains may well reinforce that belief.

Sorel invented over one hundred dishes to please her royal patron, and, like many of the women who followed her, also served as a source of inspiration to great chefs. The following dish, which was dedicated to Agnès by Adolphe Dugléré, of Paris' famed Café des Anglais, is considered one of the truly great French dishes. Although it is traditionally served as a first course, it may also be served as the main course at a light dinner

Omelette Agnès Sorel

8 eggs
¼ cup cooked boned chicken breast
3 Tbsp sweet cream
About 6 Tbsp butter

1 cup mushrooms, sliced
1 cup veal or chicken stock
16 thin slices of smoked or pickled tongue
salt and pepper to taste

In a food processor process the chicken until it is completely smooth and then blend together with the cream.

In a skillet melt 2 Tbsp of butter and in this sauté the mushrooms. Drain the excess liquids and mix the mushrooms and chicken puree together. In a saucepan heat the mixture through, dab the surface with butter and set aside to keep warm.

Boil down the veal stock to ½ of its original volume and into this blend 1–2 Tbsp of butter. Keep warm while preparing the omelets.

To prepare the omelets, lightly beat 2 of the eggs in a small bowl with a dinner fork. In a 9″ (23 cm) omelet pan melt 2 Tbsp of butter, rolling the butter over the bottom and sides of the pan. When the butter is heated through and bubbling but not yet brown, add the eggs. Agitate the pan forward and backward allowing the eggs to slide as a mass over the pan bottom just until the eggs begin to thicken. Quickly pull the egg mixture from the sides to the center of the pan so that the uncooked portion flows to the side. Continue until the omelet is nearly cooked to taste (30–50 seconds).

During the last 10–15 seconds of cooking do not stir the mixture, allowing the bottom to brown. As soon as the omelet is ready, spoon over ¼ of the chicken and mushroom mixture. To turn the omelet out, have a hot serving plate ready. Hold the pan in one hand and tip slightly towards the body. With a fork fold over the edge of the omelet nearest the handle and then half roll, half slide the omelet onto the serving plate so that it lands on the plate folded in three, folded side down. Repeat this process until all the eggs are used, making 4 omelets in all.

To serve, place 4 slices of the tongue around the omelets and over this pour a border of the reduced veal stock. (Serves 4).

Velouté Agnès Sorel
Cream of Mushroom Soup à l'Agnès Sorel

FOR THE *VELOUTÉ*:

3 oz (85 gr) flour
6 Tbsp clarified butter
8 cups chicken consommé

3 egg yolks
6 Tbsp sweet cream

FOR THE GARNISH:

½ cup Champignon
    mushrooms, sliced
2 Tbsp clarified butter
1 cup white chicken meat,
    cooked and cut into
    julienne strips

1 cup pickled tongue, sliced
    and cut into julienne strips
2–3 truffles, whole
3–4 Tbsp sweet cream
2 tsp chives, snipped

Prepare the soup: In a 2 quart soup pot melt 3 Tbsp of the clarified butter and into this mix the flour, stirring constantly over a low flame for

3–4 minutes. Add 1 cup of the chicken consommé and stir well over the flame until the mixture is completely smooth. Add the remaining consommé, heat to boiling, stirring occasionally and then remove from the heat.

In a small bowl, whisk together the egg yolks and sweet cream. Stirring constantly, add the egg yolk and cream mixture to the soup, stirring until the soup begins to thicken. Blend in 3 Tbsp of the clarified butter and stir until the mixture is completely smooth.

Prepare the garnish: In a saucepan melt the butter and in this sauté the mushroom slices for 2–3 minutes. Add the chicken and tongue and over a low flame sauté for 2–3 minutes longer.

Return the *velouté* to the heat, add the contents of the saucepan and heat through, stirring. To serve, distribute the *velouté* in 4–6 soup bowls, distributing the mushrooms, chicken and tongue evenly. Finish each portion with a swirl of ½ Tbsp of sweet cream. Over each portion grate the truffles and sprinkle over 1 tsp of the chives and serve at once. (Serves 4–6).

Martino Rossi, mid-15th century

Renaissance Man

W hat a cook, O immortal gods!" So wrote Bartolomeo Sacchi, the Italian humanist also known as Platina, about his friend, the master-cook Martino Rossi. Platina translated into Latin the recipes collected in Rossi's manuscript, *Libro de arte coquinaria*, and included them in his own *De Honesta Voluptate*, which was printed in Venice in 1475 and went through six editions by the beginning of the sixteenth century. The book was also translated into Italian, French and German, thus spreading Italian Renaissance recipes all over Europe.

Not much is known about the life of Maestro Martino, as Rossi was known. A native of Lombardy, he was born in the first half of the fifteen century and served first as cook to the duke of Milan, Francesco Sforza, and later to Cardinal Ludovico Trevisan, in Rome. Platina probably met Martino in Trevisan's villa near Rome, and would also have enjoyed his dishes at the dinners served to a small group of members of the Roman Academy.

Prior to Martino, there were no proper culinary manuals in Italy, and cooks recorded recipes primarily for themselves. In his manuscript Martino dedicates different chapters to various types of food (meats, broths, soups, pastas and sauces), specifies the number of persons that

a recipe will serve, the quantity of ingredients needed, and the method and time of cooking. In the opening paragraph of the book, for example, he writes: "the fatty meat of oxen and that of beef should be boiled, the loin should be roasted, and the haunch made into cutlets. All the meat of mutton is good boiled, except for the shoulder, which is good roasted, as is the haunch."

Martino is credited with inventing the *battuto*, a basic sauce for savory dishes consisting of sautéed onion, carrot and celery, and with introducing raisins, prunes, grapes, dates, pomegranates, and bitter oranges to flavor sauces and tortes, a practice he borrowed from Arabic cooking. He was also among the first to abandon the excessive use of spices typical of medieval cookery and to focus on enhancing the natural taste of the ingredients, and the first to introduce many dishes of vegetables that had been heretofore neglected. Martino's recipes were later adapted and incorporated into several books, among them Bartolomeo Scappi's *Opera*, published in 1570 and considered today to have been the most accomplished cookbook of the Italian Renaissance.

Torta Commune
Cheese Tarte

Take good cheese with eight eggs and with some good pork or veal fat, or butter, some whole currants, ginger, cinnamon, a little grated bread, a little fatty stock made yellow with saffron, and prepare a torta.

The following recipe is a modern adaptation that yields a cheese pie in the spirit of the original.

1 standard pie crust	5 Tbsp sugar
1 lb (225 gr) ricotta cheese	1½ tsp ginger
2 large eggs	½ tsp cinnamon
1 Tbsp butter, melted	2 Tbsp currants
1 Tbsp soft white breadcrumbs	

In a food processor blend the cheese, eggs, butter, breadcrumbs, sugar and spices until smooth. Fold in the currants.

Roll out the pastry, line a 9″ (23 cm) tart tin with it and pour in the filling. Smooth the surface and bake in a medium oven until firm and showing signs of browning (about 40 minutes). Let cool before serving. (Serves 6).

Torta di Marzapane
Marzipan Torte

Grind almonds which have stood in fresh water a day and a night and which are as carefully washed as possible, continuing sprinkling lightly with fresh water so they will not produce oil. If you want the best, add as much of the best sugar as of almonds. When all has been well pounded and soaked in rosewater, spread in a pan filled with a light undercrust and moistened often with rosewater. Put in an oven, sprinkling continually with ground sugar with a bit of rosewater so that it will not be dried too much.

The recipe that follows is a modern adaptation.

1 cup almonds, washed and soaked in water for several hours	water to assist in grinding
	1 standard pie crust for a 9″ torte
1 cup white sugar	crème fraiche for serving
4 Tbsp rosewater	

In a blender grind the almonds together with about 2 Tbsp of water. Turn into a bowl, add all but 1 Tbsp of the sugar and mix well. Add 3½ Tbsp of rosewater, mix well and let stand for 15–20 minutes.

Prepare the pastry in the normal fashion and chill before rolling out. With the pastry line the pie tin and bake blind for 15 minutes in a medium oven. Fill the crust with the almond-sugar mixture and bake for 30 minutes longer. Sprinkle over the remaining sugar and rosewater. Just before serving spoon crème fraiche over individual portions. (Serves 6).

Blackberry Sauce

Heavenly blue sauce for the summer: Take some of the wild blackberries that grow in hedgerows and some thoroughly pounded almonds, with a little ginger. And moisten these things with verjuice and strain through a sieve.

This slightly sour Cerulean blue sauce is a good accompaniment to chicken or veal dishes. Following is a modern adaptation.

¼ lb (115 gr) blackberries
⅓ cup unblanched almonds,
    ground
¼ cup verjuice or a mixture of

2½ Tbsp cider mixed with
   1½ Tbsp water
1 tsp fresh ginger, grated
1 tsp sugar
pinch of salt

In a food processor puree the blackberries. Strain the juice, pressing to extract as much of the liquid as possible.

    With a mortar and pestle or in a blender, grind the almonds and ginger together and then add these to the blackberry juice. The mixture will turn Cerulean blue. Add the verjuice and a pinch of salt, strain again and serve in a sauce bowl. (Yields about 1 cup).

Cesar & Lucrezia Borgia, 1475–1507, 1480–1519

Food for Tasting

Few families have been treated as badly by historians as the Borgias, commonly portrayed as murderers who eliminated their enemies by poison. It is true that the Borgias were vindictive people, and Cesar Borgia did not hesitate to have his or his sister's enemies excommunicated or imprisoned. However, not a single mention is to be found of their having ever poisoned anybody.

This myth started only in the nineteenth century. Oxford scholar Gregory Hardy wrote that "it was not unusual for the Borgias to eliminate as many as one or two people every week...with a white powder, *cantarela*, which was sugary and had a pleasing taste when added to a dish, but quite deadly." Alexandre Dumas, in his *Crimes Célèbres*, suggests that the Borgias forced a bear to swallow a strong dose of arsenic and, as the poison took effect, suspended the beast by his hind legs so that a stream of foam poured from its mouth. According to Dumas, this foam was then collected on a silver plate and bottled in the Vatican.

Among the wealthiest families in fifteenth and sixteenth century Italy, the Borgias entertained lavishly. A cardinal and a soldier in the service of the Vatican, Cesar Borgia hosted grand dinners in his palatial homes in Rome, Florence and Ferrara, often inviting as many as five hundred guests for eight or ten course dinners. After dining with him in 1497, the Duke of Tuscany wrote to his wife that in addition to serving "food that was inedible, the man himself is terrible. He passes air, sneezes and wheezes, scratches himself and blows his nose at table." Worst of all, it was said that Cesar was an impossible chatterer, never giving his guests a chance to say a word.

Despite his lack of etiquette, Cesar had the ear not only of the pope but of a collection of kings, and had many followers, as did his far more refined sister, the beautiful Lucrezia, Duchess of Ferrara. Whether in her castle in Ferrara or her home in Rome, it was her habit to host intimate dinners at least three times every week. Her parties were considered great successes, partly due to her chef, Gregorio Platini, one of the most talented chefs of the time.

Cesar and Lucrezia were both terrified of being poisoned and therefore employed food tasters. Since not all poisons act quickly, the tasters had to eat their samples half an hour before the Borgias dined, and while none of the tasters ever died of poisoning, this practice assured that every dish the Borgias consumed was quite cold by the time they finally got to it.

According to popular folklore, the following dish was invented by Cristoforo di Zeffirano, a Bolognese chef, who dedicated it to Lucrezia on the occasion of her wedding to the Duke of Ferrara, Alfonso d'Este, in 1501.

Torta di Porro alla Borgia
Leek Tart alla Borgia

¼ lb (115 gr) leeks, white parts only
½ cup butter, softened
3 cups flour

1¼ cups milk, warm
½ cup Parmesan cheese, grated
2 egg yolks
salt and pepper to taste

Wash the leeks well, cook them in lightly salted boiling water for 10 minutes, and drain. In a heavy skillet melt 2 Tbsp of the butter and in this sauté the leeks over a low flame for 4–5 minutes.

In a saucepan melt 2 Tbsp of the remaining butter and into this stir ¼ cup of the flour, mixing thoroughly. To this mixture, slowly add the milk, stirring constantly until the sauce is smooth and without lumps. Remove from the flame and season to taste with pepper. Whisk in the Parmesan cheese and egg yolks and set the sauce aside.

Place the remaining flour in a mixing bowl and make a well in the center. Add the remaining butter, a pinch or two of salt and 1 Tbsp of cold water. Work this mixture into smooth soft dough, adding a bit of water if necessary. Roll the dough into a circle large enough to line a lightly buttered 9″ (23 cm) pie tin with sides about 2″ (5 cm) high. Bake blind by filling the tart with uncooked rice and baking in a medium oven for 20 minutes. Remove the rice (which may be cooked in the usual way any time in the future).

Arrange the leeks in a neat row on the pastry and over the leeks pour the sauce. Return to the oven and bake for 20–25 minutes longer. Let the pie stand for 2–3 minutes before sliding it out onto a serving platter and serving. (Serves 6 as a first course).

Mont Blanc aux Marons
Chestnut Mount Blanc

Although this famous dessert, based on a sweetened puree of chestnuts piled high with whipped cream, is considered an integral part of classic French cuisine, it probably originated in Italy. The dish is first mentioned in Platina's *De Honesta Voluptate* which was printed in Venice in 1475, sponsored by the Borgias, and the first actual recipe, nearly identical to the one used today, appears in Bartolomeo Scappi's *Opera*, published in 1570.

In 1620, a baker in Chamonix, France, credited the dessert to himself, and once it had been established as a French recipe, the burghers of Paris, Lyon and Grenoble adopted it as their own. Today, it is known even in Italy by its French name.

3¼ lb (1½ kilos) chestnuts
1 cup + 2 Tbsp sugar
3 cups milk
1 vanilla bean, about 2″ (5 cm)
    long

2 Tbsp butter
¼ tsp salt
1½ cups sweet cream, well
    chilled
2–3 drops vanilla extract

To prepare the chestnuts, cut a cross in the top of each and set them in a saucepan of cold water. Bring to the boil, boil for 1 minute and remove from the flame. Drain the chestnuts, pour over cold water to cover and, before the chestnuts become completely cool, peel off and discard the outer and inner skins.

In the top of a double boiler scald the milk together with ¼ cup of the sugar and the vanilla bean. Add the peeled chestnuts and cook over boiling water until the chestnuts are very tender (about 30 minutes). Drain the chestnuts and puree them in a food mill or with a sieve. (Do not discard the milk as it may be used later to make puddings or sweet rice desserts).

To make sugar syrup, mix ¾ cup of the remaining sugar with 6 Tbsp of water and boil, stirring regularly, until a temperature of 230 degrees Fahrenheit (110 degrees Celsius) is obtained. Add the sugar syrup, butter and salt to the chestnut puree and then force through a ricer or a wire sieve, letting the vermicelli-like puree fall into a 9″ (23 cm) ring mold. Turn the mold over on a chilled serving plate and place in the refrigerator. Let chill thoroughly before serving.

Pour the sweet cream into a completely dry chilled bowl and beat it by hand or with an electric beater until the cream is stiff enough to form soft peaks when the beater is lifted out. If the cream is not to be used immediately it may be stored in the refrigerator for up to two hours. Just before serving, fold in the sugar and vanilla extract and then fill the center of the chestnut ring with the cream, shaping the cream into a dome. (Serves 8–10).

François Rabelais, 1483–1553

In Praise of Gluttony

A monk, physician and writer remembered for his satirical romances *Gargantua* and *Pantagruel*, François Rabelais was also a revered cook and gourmand, who celebrated the culinary joys in his books, including sharing sixty ways to cook an egg. In *Gargantua* he writes, "Drink always and you shall never die."

The giant Gargantua was born after his mother ate too much tripe, exploded, and expelled her son through her ear. His father, Grandgousier (literally, big gullet) would feast in one dinner on hams, beef tongues, salted beef with mustard, salted roe, and a larder full of sausages, and Gargantua himself once ate six innocent pilgrims in his lettuce salad as a first course before his supper. In the morning Gargantua "crapped, pissed, threw up, belched, yawned, farted, spat, coughed, sobbed, sneezed, blew his nose like an archdeacon and ate breakfast to put down the bad air: fine dried tripe, beautiful carbonadoes, fair hams, fine game stews, and many early morning dips as snacks."

Rabelais was born near the town of Chinon, France. Although most historians agree that he was born in 1483, others date his birth to 1490 or 1495. He became a Franciscan monk in the convent of Gontenay-le-Comte, where he remained for fifteen years, until he entered the Benedictine abbey of Maillezais. He studied medicine in Montpellier, became a physician at the Hôtel-Dieu hospital in Lyons and in 1532 published *Pantagruel*, which was followed two years later by *Gargantua*. Rabelais took the character of Gargantua from a booklet of folk tales which was sold in Lyons, and elaborated the adventures of this giant in a series of four books. A fifth was published after his death in 1553, but its authorship is disputed.

The narrator of these outrageous and subversive texts rejects any institutional order and celebrates the physical joys of life—food, drink, sex, and the bodily functions connected to them. He was acclaimed by Chateaubriand as the founder of French letters, while Voltaire described his work as "a heap of the most impertinent and gross filth a monk could vomit." The books were highly successful, despite the fact that they were condemned by the Sorbonne and the French Parliament, and were listed in the index of forbidden books of the Catholic Church.

Rabelais' work is valuable for gastronomes since it contains wonderful lists of dishes, utensils and recipes, as, for example, the brioche-like cake called *fouace* or *fougasse* over which Lerne, the king with the bitter bile, starts a war against Gargantua. Rabelais's recipe includes butter, egg yolks, saffron, and other spices. The cake is traditionally served in France during the celebration of Easter. Another famous recipe of Rabelais is for Bishop's testicles, which, for obvious reasons, is not replicated here.

Fouace Rabelais
Easter Brioche

3 cups flour, sifted
1 envelope dried yeast mixed
    with 2 Tbsp sugar
lukewarm water as required
1 tsp salt
6 Tbsp lukewarm milk
1 tsp orange-flower water (if
    unavailable use a pinch

each of ground lemon rind
    and cinnamon)
⅛ tsp saffron, soaked in
    lukewarm water for 1 hour
4 eggs, lightly beaten
½ lb (225 gr) + 1 Tbsp butter at
    room temperature
1 egg yolk

In a mixing bowl combine 1 cup of the sifted flour with the yeast and sugar mixture. Add just enough lukewarm water to form a small, soft ball of dough. Cut a cross in the top of this starter dough and immerse it in a bowl of lukewarm water.

Dissolve the salt in 3 Tbsp of the milk.

Place the remaining flour on a dry working surface. Make a well in the center and into this pour the salt and milk solution, orange-flower water, saffron and lightly beaten eggs. Gradually gather the flour from the edges of the well into the eggs to make a soft batter.

Meanwhile, turn back to the first ball of dough. Wait until it has floated to the surface of the water, lift it out with one hand, allowing the water to drop back into the bowl, and mix the batter and starter together.

Divide the ½ lb (225 gr) of the butter into four segments, place these on different sides of the dough and with the fingertips slowly work each portion of butter into the dough by twisting the dough and pulling it from the countertop. When the dough is uniform set it aside to let rise, covered with a tea towel in a warm place. Let the dough rise for 6–8 hours, punching it down whenever it reaches the top of the mixing bowl. Cover with plastic wrap and refrigerate overnight.

Butter an oven pan or firm cookie sheet. With your hands roll out the brioche dough to form a tube about 12–14″ (30–35 cm) long. Form the roll into a circle and press the ends closed. With a sharp knife cut small incisions about ¾″ (2 cm) deep at regular intervals and let the dough stand to rise again until 1½ times its original volume. Mix the egg yolk with the remaining milk and with this brush the bread. Bake in an oven preheated to hot. Bake until nicely browned (about 20 minutes). (Serves 12).

Catherine de Medici, 1519–1589
The Florentine Touch

Historians will argue forever about the extent of the contribution of Catherine de Medici to French cuisine, but there is no question that she altered the dining habits of the French by introducing them to truffles, Parmesan cheese, artichokes, broccoli and milk-fed veal, as well as delicacies such as quenelles, Zabaglione, duck in orange sauce and various pastas. She also suggested the use of the fork, but this proved too progressive for the French, who were to reject the concept for nearly a century longer.

When she arrived in France in 1533, at the age of fourteen, to marry the future King Henri II, Catherine was dismayed at the poor quality of French cookery. Luckily, she had brought with her a small entourage of Florentine cooks and confectioners, who supplied her table with sorbets and ice creams, marmalades, fruits in syrup, pastries and pasta. Catherine instituted new dining protocols, such as the separation of salty and sweet dishes at a time when sweets were still consumed together with meat and fish, the attendance of women at dinners, and an elegance in service unseen before her time. Venetian glassware, porcelain and luxurious silverware were the rule for her dinners, and all in all she created a new style for royal banqueting that would achieve its

royal guest commented that "with gifts such as these there should never again be found a reason to go to war with our southern neighbors."

Today, only two dishes bear her name, both desserts. The first is a dish that Catherine is said to have invented herself, the second, an ice cream bombe, was prepared in honor of her seventieth birthday. There is probably no recipe in the world more fattening or richer in cholesterol than this, and on sampling it Catherine said that "after having tasted something so wondrous, one may be comfortably assured that there is indeed a Paradise that awaits us." Several hours later she died in her sleep, reportedly "with a smile on her lips."

Poires Catherine

Pears Catherine

8 pears
4½ cups sugar
1 tsp vanilla extract (or more
    to taste)

4 cups raspberries or
    blackberries
2 Tbsp kirsch liqueur
3 Tbsp almonds, chopped
    finely
Chantilly cream (optional)

Prepare sugar syrup by dissolving 4 cups of the sugar in 4½ cups of water and bringing to a boil. Strain, add the vanilla and filter through several layers of muslin. Pour the syrup into a clean saucepan and in this poach the pears until they are soft, taking care not to cook so long that they become mushy.

In a mixing bowl crush the berries (if using tinned berries be sure to drain and discard the liquids in the tin). Add the remaining sugar, mix well, and put through a sieve. Stir in the kirsch. To serve, spoon the berry puree over the pears and sprinkle over with the almonds. Serve with Chantilly cream in a separate bowl if so desired. (Serves 4).

Bombe Medicis

4 cups pear or orange sorbet	6 large peaches, halved and
2 cups peaches, peeled and	peeled
diced	32 egg yolks
½ cup kirsch liqueur	1 tsp vanilla extract
8½ cups sugar	3 cups sweet cream, whipped
	stiff

Line a bombe mold or earthenware bowl with the sorbet and place in the freezer until solidified.

In a small bowl steep the diced peaches in the kirsch for 1–2 hours.

In a small saucepan dissolve 1½ cups of the sugar in 2 cups of water and bring to the boil. In this syrup simmer the peach halves until soft. Drain and puree the peaches.

In a saucepan dissolve the remaining sugar in 4 cups of water. Bring to a rolling boil, strain and filter. Combine the syrup and egg yolks in the top of a large double boiler, over, but not in, hot water, stirring regularly with a whisk. When the mixture attains the consistency of thick cream rub it through a fine sieve into a bowl. Add the vanilla extract and continue to stir until the mixture is fully cool. Add to the mixture the peach puree and diced peaches and then add an equal volume of the whipped cream. Place the mixture in a stone or porcelain container, cover and refrigerate until completely cold (4–5 hours).

When the mixture is cold fill the center of the bombe. Seal the mold and let stand in the freezer until solid throughout (about 2 hours) before unmolding and serving. (Serves 12–16).

Queen Elizabeth I, 1533–1603

A Stomach of a King

More than any other culinary offerings, Queen Elizabeth I loved sweets—cookies, candies and *petits fours* that she stored in large pockets sewn into all of her dresses. In fact, she ate so much sugar that her teeth turned black.

"I know I have the body of a weak and feeble woman, but I have the heart and stomach of a king, and of a king of England too," she said. Demonstrating the capacity of her stomach was one of the queen's great pleasures, for Good Queen Bess, as she was affectionately known, enjoyed the wealth and grandeur of the banquet table not only in her palaces but at the estates of her subjects throughout the country.

Every year on August 25th, the Queen would leave her palace in London to go on "progresses"—a series of trips throughout her kingdom that were meant to enhance her popularity. In September of 1578 she visited the estate of Lord North, in Kirtling, Cambridgeshire, accompanied by an entourage of nearly three hundred people. Lord North's account books show that in anticipation of the glorious event he purchased "a cartload and two horse loads of oysters, 650 kilos of the finest beef, 400 kilos of butter, 500 liters of sweet cream and 4,522 eggs." He also built a special house for the guests and hired additional cooks

from London to augment the eighty-two people already on his regular serving and kitchen staff. He presented the Queen with a jewel worth one hundred and twenty pounds, about twelve thousand pounds in today's terms, and bought gifts for her courtiers and servants.

The honor of entertaining and feeding the Queen cost Lord North 762 pounds, over 75,000 pounds in today's terms. Such generosity frequently paid off, not only in gifts of land or titles but also in other royal favors. Years later, when Elizabeth heard that Lord North was suffering from an ear infection, she offered him her own prescription: "Bake a loaf of bean flour and when it is still hot cut it into halves. Into each half pour three or four spoonfuls of bitter almond extract then place both halves to your ears before going to bed."

The dinner Lord North served to the queen and her party consisted of smoked sturgeon, chicken stuffed with bacon and oysters, roasted quails, lamb with cucumbers, venison pie, boiled beef with sauce Robert, and pears in syrup and apple cream, which was the queen's favorite dessert. The meal also introduced two new contributions to the dining habits of the day; the first was a replacement for trenchers, those thick slices of bread used as plates and then thrown to the dogs at tableside, by square wooden bowls that had been carved with separate hollow portions for meat, gravy and other side dishes. The queen is reported to have found these new plates "amusing." The second innovation, the two pronged fork, was rejected by the queen, who thought it fit only for prudish women. She continued to eat with her fingers.

Lamb with Cucumbers

1 shoulder of lamb, about 6½
    lb (3 kilos), with the bone
    removed
1 tsp mace
2 Tbsp olive oil
2 Tbsp butter
½ lb (225 gr) mushrooms,
    chopped finely
4 shallots, chopped finely
2 onions, chopped finely
1 cup breadcrumbs

¾ tsp each thyme and
    marjoram
½ tsp each savory and tarragon
2 Tbsp parsley, chopped
1 egg, lightly beaten
½ cup butter
1½ cups beef stock
8 cucumbers
2–3 Tbsp flour
juice of ½ lemon
salt and pepper to taste

Season the lamb with salt, pepper and mace. In a flameproof casserole dish heat the olive oil and butter and in this sauté the mushrooms, shallots and half the onions. Remove from the flame and mix in the breadcrumbs, herbs, half the parsley and the egg. Lay the meat out flat and cover one side with this mixture and then tie the meat neatly.

To the casserole dish add 3 Tbsp of the butter. Heat through and brown the meat and remaining onions in the butter (brown the meat on all sides). Pour over 1 cup of the stock, cover and place in a medium-hot oven until the meat is medium-rare (about 1½ hours).

Peel and cut the cucumbers into 2″ (5 cm) sticks. Place these in a bowl and sprinkle generously with salt. Let stand ½ hour and then gently press out the water. Roll the cucumbers in flour that has been seasoned with pepper and fry them in the remaining butter until they are golden brown.

Remove the meat from the casserole dish and carve. To the casserole disk, add the remaining stock and the lemon juice, and heat through, scraping the bottom and sides of the casserole dish. To serve, place the cucumbers to one side of the meat, pour over the sauce from the casserole dish, and sprinkle over the remaining parsley. (Serves 6–8).

Apple Cream

8 apples, peeled, cored and
    quartered
1½ cups sugar
2 cups rosé wine
rind of 1 lemon

pinch each of dried rosemary
    and thyme
1 envelope gelatin
½ cup sweet Sherry wine
1 cup sweet cream, whipped
    stiff

Place the apples in a saucepan with the sugar, rosé wine, lemon rind, rosemary and thyme. Simmer until the apples are very soft. Strain and reserve the wine. Puree the apples through a fine strainer into a bowl and then add the reserved wine.

In the top of a double boiler, soak the gelatin in the Sherry for 5 minutes and then melt over hot water. Add the gelatin to the apples. Stir well and let the mixture cool.

When the apple mixture begins to stiffen, fold in the whipped cream. Pour into a mold that has been rinsed in cold water and chill in the refrigerator until firm. Unmold just before serving. (Serves 6–8).

King Henri IV, 1553–1610

The Great Béarnaise

Henri IV was not the wisest of kings. To his credit, on his ascension to the throne in 1589, he did put an end to the civil war that had been tearing France apart. However, he also involved France in three unsuccessful wars, alienated the monarchs of nearly every other European nation, and was so extravagant in his personal life that he bankrupted the national treasury. Despite all this, the French remember him even today with extraordinary fondness, having bestowed on him the title *Le Bon Roi Henri*.

Whatever else he was, Henri was a man devoted to excellent dining. He felt that it was the "moral obligation of all French men and women to dine well at least three times daily" and promised to supply every French home with a large black kettle. "If God allows me to live, I will see that there is not a single laborer in my kingdom who does not have a chicken in his pot every Sunday," he wrote.

The king rarely kept his promises, but most gastronomes are willing to forgive him that sin because of his great gift to the world of gastronomy: his patronage over one of the oldest inns in Europe, La Tour d'Argent. Seven years before he ascended the throne, in 1582, the very same year this elegant inn had opened its doors between the

Seine and the Bernardins Monastery, the future king stopped there for refreshments.

The inn, originally reserved exclusively for aristocrats, was built in the Renaissance style, from stone with silver detail, its décor boasted carved buffets, tiled floors, tapestries, linen maps and pewter goblets. Among the dishes served there were eggs of salted mullet, soup Lyonnaise and pork pastries for starters, followed by all kinds of rich roasts. The dauphin was so pleased with the food there that when he became king of France he presented the restaurant with a coat of arms, thus distinguishing it from all the other taverns of Paris.

By 1600, La Tour d'Argent was so fashionable that duels were fought to obtain a table there. Henri IV would send to the Tour d'Argent for thick slices of Heron Pâté and the Duke of Richelieu treated his guests to a whole ox prepared in thirty different ways. Coffee and chocolate drinks were introduced there for the first time and in 1890 the famous Frédéric created the ritual of the "Canard au Sang" and decreed that each duck would bear a number. Since then, every Caneton Tour d'Argent has been registered.

The Tour d'Argent's prestige, along with its regal prices, continues to this day. The following dish was dedicated to the king by an unknown chef at the world-famous establishment in 1820.

Tournedos Henri IV

4 tournedos, about 1½" (4 cm)
   thick
1 lb (450 gr) potatoes, peeled
   and cut in 1" (2½ cm) balls
1 cup butter
4 large artichoke hearts
½ lemon
4 thick slices white bread,
   without crusts
1 Tbsp olive oil
¼ cup Madeira wine
¼ cup veal or beef stock

¼ cup porcini or chanterelle
   mushrooms, sliced
salt and pepper to taste
¾ cup Béarnaise sauce (recipe
   follows)

In a large amount of lightly salted boiling water cook the potato balls until nearly tender. Drain and set aside. Several minutes before serving the dish, melt ¼ cup of the butter in a skillet and in this sauté the potatoes until nicely browned.

Rub the artichoke hearts with the lemon. In a saucepan with about 1″ (2½ cm) of boiling water cook the hearts until tender (about 20 minutes). Drain and set aside to keep warm.

Cut the bread slices so that they are about the same size as the steaks. In a large skillet melt 2 Tbsp of the butter and in this fry the bread slices until golden brown on both sides. Set them aside to keep warm.

Add 2 Tbsp of the remaining butter to the skillet and in this sauté the mushrooms just until they are tender (3–4 minutes). Remove the mushrooms with a slotted spoon, drain and set aside to keep warm.

Add the olive oil and 2 Tbsp of the remaining butter to the skillet and heat over a medium flame. Dry the steaks on paper toweling and when the oil and butter mixture is very hot place the steaks in the skillet and sauté them for 3–4 minutes on each side. Place the steaks on the toast slices and set aside to keep warm.

Pour the excess fat out of the skillet, add the Madeira and stock and boil the mixture rapidly, scraping the bottom and sides of the skillet constantly, until the mixture is reduced to about 3 Tbsp. Spoon this mixture over the steaks and on each steak place an artichoke heart. Fill the artichoke hearts with the Béarnaise sauce and decorate the plate with the potatoes and mushrooms.

Sauce Béarnaise

As Henri IV came from the area known as Béarn, he was sometimes known as The Great Béarnaise. The first recipe for the sauce that carries his name appeared in a book published in 1818. Baron Brisse, a well known banker of the day, wrote of this sauce that "it frightens me. Merely reading the recipe arouses my hunger and with it one might never stop eating."

2 Tbsp wine vinegar

2 Tbsp dry white wine

½ Tbsp shallots, chopped very finely

1½ tsp dried tarragon

pinch or two of pepper

pinch of salt

2 egg yolks

2 Tbsp butter (cold)

½ cup butter, melted

2 Tbsp parsley, chopped very finely

In a small saucepan combine the vinegar, wine, shallots, tarragon and salt and pepper and heat over a medium flame until the liquid has been reduced to 1 Tbsp Set aside and let cool to room temperature.

In a saucepan beat the egg yolks until they are thick. Strain in the vinegar mixture and beat for 1–2 minutes. Add 1 Tbsp of the cold butter and place over a low flame, stirring until the butter has completely melted. Beat in the other tablespoon of cold butter in the same way. Drop by drop add the melted butter, beating constantly until the mixture is completely smooth. Correct the seasoning with salt and pepper to taste and then beat in the parsley. If not using immediately, put a pat of butter on a fork and with this coat the surface of the sauce. (Yields about ¾ cup).

Cardinal Richelieu, 1585–1642

Bitter Tastes

Born Armand-Jean du Plessis, Cardinal Richelieu served as chief minister to Louis XIII from 1624 until his death. Even though he was, in fact, the most powerful man in France, he is remembered today mainly as the arch-villain and master of political intrigue in Dumas' *Les Trois Mousquetaires*. Historians, however, consider him to have been the father of the modern nation-state, and claim that his efforts to consolidate royal power paved the way for the absolute monarchy of King Louis XIV. He is also remembered as a patron of the arts, the founder of the *Académie Française*, and the constructor of what is today the *Palais Royal*.

As a host, Richelieu gave sumptuous dinners. He is said to have been the first in France to make use of the table knife. It is also said that it was he who ordered the heads of his knives to be rounded off from their previous sharp points, so that none of his guests could stab him. Historian Sanche de Gramont wrote that "no Frenchman before or after Richelieu has ever had as many enemies." Richelieu himself is reported to have said, "if you give me six lines written by the most honest man, I would find something in them to have him hanged."

Wherever the Cardinal went he was accompanied by three

bodyguards and an official taster who sampled his food. Among the culinary treats credited to Richelieu is hot chocolate, a beverage not consumed in France until he made it popular. It is said that the Cardinal learned about the drink from his brother, who is known to have used chocolate for medicinal purposes.

Richelieu lived to be fifty-seven, but his taster, a Corsican named Philippe Gravier, outlived him and died at the age of ninety-eight. After Richelieu's death, Gravier returned to his native island, there to open a tavern in the village of Alleria. That tavern, now a small hotel and restaurant, is where the family of Gravier still proudly holds court.

Foie Gras Richelieu
Goose Liver à la Richelieu

FOR THE MAITRE D'HOTEL BUTTER:

¼ cup butter, at room temperature
½ tsp salt
¼ tsp white pepper
1 tsp parsley, chopped finely
1 Tbsp lemon juice

FOR THE FOIE GRAS:

8 slices of goose liver
butter as required
6 large mushroom caps, sliced
    thinly

breadcrumbs as required
salt and pepper to taste
2 eggs beaten with 1 Tbsp
    water

Make the maitre d'hotel butter: With a wooden spoon, cream the butter. Add the salt, pepper and parsley and blend in thoroughly. Stirring constantly, add the lemon juice very slowly, mixing in well. Refrigerate and use only when the butter has become solid.

Prepare the foie gras: In a small skillet melt 2 Tbsp of the butter and in this sauté the mushroom slices just until heated through.

    Season the breadcrumbs with salt and pepper. Dip the goose liver slices first in the eggs and then in the breadcrumbs, coating well. In a heavy skillet melt 2 Tbsp of the butter and in this fry the slices until golden brown on both sides (add more butter only if the skillet becomes dry). To serve, garnish the foie gras with the mushrooms and on each slice place several dabs of the maitre d'hotel butter. (Serves 8 as a first course).

Note: This dish may also be made using fillets of sole or boneless chicken breasts that have been pounded flat.

Richelieu
Richelieu Cake

FOR THE CAKE:

3 cups almonds, pounded finely
2 egg whites
10 egg whites, beaten stiff
2¼ cups sugar
16 egg yolks

¼ cup maraschino liqueur
½ cup butter, melted
1½ cups flour, sifted
few drops of vanilla extract
1 cup apricot jam

FOR THE FRANGIPANE CREAM:

1½ cups sugar
1 cup flour, sifted
pinch of salt
2 eggs and 2 egg yolks
4 tsp vanilla extract

½ tsp almond extract
2 cups boiling milk
½ cup butter, melted
1 cup almonds, finely crushed
¼ cup kirsch liqueur

FOR THE CHOCOLATE ICING:

½ lb (225 gr) semisweet
    chocolate
2 Tbsp butter
1 tsp vanilla extract

pinch or two of salt
2 cups confectioners' sugar,
    sifted
⅓ cup milk

Make the cake: In a mixing bowl combine the almonds and unbeaten egg whites with ¼ cup of the sugar. Mix well and rub through a sieve into a large bowl. Add the remaining sugar, egg yolks and maraschino liqueur and mix with a wooden spoon until the mixture is white. Add the melted butter, sprinkle in the flour and fold in the beaten egg whites, mixing well. Divide the mixture equally between 4 shallow buttered 20 cm. baking pans and bake in a medium oven until an inserted tooth-pick comes out clean. Turn out to cool on a rack.

Make the frangipane cream: In a heavy saucepan combine the sugar, flour and salt. Add the eggs and egg yolks, vanilla extract and almond extract and mix well. Mixing constantly, slowly add the milk. Cook over a low flame, stirring constantly, for 2–3 minutes. Remove from the flame, add the butter, crushed almonds and the kirsch, and mix thoroughly.

Make the chocolate icing: Melt the chocolate in the top of a double boiler until completely melted. Add the butter, vanilla and salt and then mix together with the sugar, beating hard with a wooden spoon, adding just enough milk to make the icing thick and of a good spreading consistency.

On three of the cake layers spread apricot jam and then a layer of the Frangipane cream. Sandwich the layers together. On the top layer spread the remaining jam and ice the cake with the chocolate icing. (Serves 6–8).

François Pierre de La Varenne, 1618–1678

Magic in the Saucepan

The son of a farmer from Burgundy who had been imprisoned because he could not pay his debts, François Pierre de La Varenne was to become the most influential culinary authority of seventeen century France. It is believed he acquired his training in the kitchens of Marie de Medici, the wife of King Henri I V, and by the 1640s he was already *chef de cuisine* to the Marquis d'Uxelle, to whom he dedicated his books and the famous mushroom duxelles. Curnonsky, the great twentieth century gourmet, observed "that without La Varenne's discovery of duxelles, French cuisine would be a mere shadow, a non-entity, nothing worthy of note."

La Varenne was acknowledged as a supreme *sauciere*, a great logician of menu planning, and a master baker. In 1651 he published *Le Cuisinier Francais*, the first French cookbook in two hundred years, and a gastronomic landmark. In that work La Varenne established the foundations of an authentic French cuisine and made a clear break from the Italian tradition that dominated French cookery in the sixteenth century. He abandoned the earlier heavy, over-spiced dishes and introduced a subtler, simpler style of cooking with natural tastes, vegetable and fruit dishes, and a whole new cuisine based on butter, bouillon and *roux*. La Varenne is also credited with the introduction of Béchamel sauce, the first bisque, and the first basic Hollandaise sauce.

The book marked the process by which France became "a culinary world apart," writes food historian Joan DeJean, and indeed, it was at that time that Paris became the international capital of gastronomy, where sweet dishes, previously part of every course, were shifted to the end of the meal, and French cuisine as we now know it began to take shape.

Duxelles

This is a recipe so versatile that it is regularly used in the preparation of first courses, soups, vegetables and garnishes. It may also be used in stuffing fish, poultry and meats, as well as in making sauces and stocks.

¼ lb (115 gr) mushrooms
   (including the stems),
   chopped finely
2 Tbsp clarified butter

½ onion, chopped finely
2 shallots, chopped
salt and pepper to taste

Place the chopped mushrooms in a clean cloth, fold over and squeeze out as much of the liquids as possible.

    In a skillet, melt the butter and in this sauté the onion until lightly browned. Add the mushrooms and shallots and stirring often over a high flame, continue to sauté until the mushrooms are cooked (5–6 minutes). Season to taste with salt and pepper. May be stored for 2–3 weeks if placed in a tightly closed jar and refrigerated. Use as instructed in the specific recipes that follow or in recipes of your own devising. (Yields about 1 cup).

Caneton Farci aux Duxelles
Duckling Stuffed with Duxelles

¼ cup Madeira wine
2 recipes for duxelles (see
   recipe above)
¼ cup breadcrumbs
3 Tbsp cream cheese
1 Tbsp butter, at room
   temperature

2 Tbsp parsley, chopped finely
½ tsp tarragon, chopped finely
1 duckling, about 3½ lbs (1½
   kilos)
salt and pepper
   to taste

In a heavy skillet pour the wine over the *duxelles* and bring to a boil, stirring constantly, until the mixture is completely dry. Remove from the flame and blend in the remaining ingredients. Correct the seasoning with salt and pepper to taste and let cool before stuffing and trussing the bird.

Rinse the duck under cold water and then dry with paper toweling. Rub the bird inside and out with salt and pepper, stuff with the *duxelles* and roast in a hot oven, basting occasionally with the drippings until the bird is done (about 30–40 minutes). Let cool for 15–20 minutes before carving. (Serves 4).

Filets de Sole aux Duxelles
Fillets of Sole with Duxelles

2 lb (900 gr) sole fillets
flour as required
3 cups duxelles
½ cup tomato sauce
1½ Tbsp olive oil

1½ Tbsp butter
2 Tbsp parsley, chopped
lemon wedges for serving
salt and pepper to taste

Season the fillets with salt and pepper and then dredge lightly with flour. In a heavy skillet heat together the oil and butter and in this sauté the fillets until done.

In a mixing bowl combine the duxelles with half the tomato sauce and mix gently but well. If the mixture seems dry, add more tomato sauce, just until the mixture is moist but not runny. Distribute the duxelles on a preheated serving platter and on this arrange the fish. Sprinkle over the parsley and pour over the oil and butter that remains in the skillet in which the fish was fried. Serve with the lemon wedges. (Serves 4–6).

Sauce Duxelles

This sauce goes marvelously with grilled steaks, chops, chicken or spooned over hard boiled eggs.

⅔ cup *demi-glace* or Espagnole
    sauce (see p. 94)
½ cup Madeira wine
½ cup white wine

½ cup tomato puree
½ cup duxelles
1 Tbsp parsley

In a small but heavy saucepan bring the brown sauce to a boil and let boil down to half. Add the Madeira wine, return to the boil and let boil 3 minutes longer. Remove from the flame.

In a separate saucepan stir together the wine and *duxelles*. Bring to a boil and let boil down until the liquids are almost absorbed. Add the brown sauce and tomato puree and boil for about 1 minute longer. Stir in the parsley and spoon over the meat or eggs being served. (Yields about 1 cup).

Jean-Baptiste Colbert, *1619–1683*

Fresh Tastes

As France's Minister of Finance under King Louis XIV, Jean-Baptiste Colbert stated that haute couture was among France's most valuable assets, and is known to have observed that "the great designers for fashion must become to France what gold mines are to Peru." He also believed that for his nation to earn the respect of the world, it should prove that its was the finest cuisine. Colbert was truly dedicated to both of these ideas. He was supportive of French acquisitions in Quebec and Louisiana because although he could see no way "to convince the savages that inhabit those lands to buy our fashionable frocks," he saw the colonies as sources for enriching the French larder.

Colbert was intrigued with the products of the New World—such as corn, sweet potatoes, squash and chocolate, but was delighted above all when French chefs started devising recipes for turkey, which he described as "large, ugly birds that smell so bad when they are alive but taste so marvelous once our good chefs have finished with them."

In his private life, Colbert's passions were divided equally between gourmet food, wine and women. "I enjoy nothing more," he wrote to a friend, "than making love, dining well and drinking the rich red wines of Bordeaux, and I am never more pleased when I can carry out these

activities all at the same time." It may well be that it was this reputation that linked his name to more than thirty well-known dishes.

Truit Colbert
Trout Colbert

4 trout
¼ cup Colbert butter (see
  following recipe)
2 small bunches parsley
3 eggs, beaten lightly with
  1 Tbsp water

1 cup dried breadcrumbs,
  seasoned with salt, pepper
  and paprika to taste
oil for deep frying

Split the trout along their backs and remove the spines. Place the eggs in a small bowl and the seasoned breadcrumbs on a flat plate. Dip the trout into the eggs and then dip in the breadcrumbs, coating well. Set aside.

Wash the parsley thoroughly, dry on paper toweling and separate into small sprigs. Place these in a wire basket and dip into deep hot oil for about 30 seconds. Drain on paper toweling.

Fry the trout in the hot oil until the fish are crisp and golden brown. Drain, transfer to a preheated serving plate and on each trout place 1 Tbsp of the Colbert butter. Garnish each end of the plate with the fried parsley. (Serves 4).

Note: This recipe can also be made using sole fillets.

Beurre Colbert
Colbert Butter

This versatile butter mixture is ideal for use with fried and grilled fish and with small cuts of meat.

1 cup beef or veal stock

1 cup butter, at room temperature

1½ Tbsp parsley, chopped finely

2 tsp tarragon, chopped finely

1 tsp lemon juice

½ tsp salt

¼ tsp pepper

In a saucepan, boil down the meat stock until it is reduced to thick syrup (there should be about 2 Tbsp left in all). Remove from the flame and add all of the remaining ingredients, stirring with a wooden spoon until the mixture forms a completely smooth paste. If not to be used at once, the Colbert butter may be packed tightly into a container, covered with plastic wrap and refrigerated for 2–3 days.

To serve Colbert butter with fish, let the butter come to room temperature before spooning it over. To serve with lamb chops, steaks or other small cuts of meat, place a generous tablespoon of the cold butter on the hot meat. As it melts it will make its own sauce. (Yields about 1 cup).

Louis de Bechameil, 1630–1703

A Lucky Fellow

Few subjects are more open to debate than the origins of Béchamel, the white sauce that is one of the four mother sauces of France's haute cuisine. Several historians trace the sauce to Cesena, a small village in the Emilia-Romagna region of Italy where *balsamella* sauce was devised to celebrate the departure of the unpopular cardinal Albornoz in the fourteenth century. Others claim that the sauce originated in the Florentine kitchens of the Medici family, and was brought to France by the cooks of Marie de Medici on the occasion of her wedding to the Duke of Orleans and future King Henri II in 1533, and that it was based on a face mask of milk and flour used by genteel Italian women.

Some suggest that the sauce was introduced only in the seventeenth century by the Duke de Mornay, who is also credited with Sauce Chasseur and Sauce Mornay, and yet more believe it is the invention of Louis de Bechameil, the Marquis de Nointel, a financier and bon vivant who served as chancellor to King Louis XIV and is said to have devised the sauce to complement dry cod. The prevailing opinion, however, is that the sauce, at least as it is known today, was named in honor of Bechameil by a court chef, possibly the great Francois Pierre de La Varenne, who included the sauce in his 1651 book *Le Cuisinier*

Francais. It is known that one of Bechameil's acquaintances, the Duke of Escasse, protested that "this fellow Bechameil has all the luck. I was serving breast of chicken *à la crème* more than twenty years before he was born, but I have never had the chance of giving my name to even the most modest sauce."

Sauce Béchamel is one of the very few French sauces that is easy to prepare, and is flavorful and delicate enough to serve on its own or as the basis for some fifty more complex sauces. Originally made by adding generous amounts of fresh cream to a thick *velouté*, the sauce is now made by whisking scalded milk into a white flour-butter *roux*. It is widely used with vegetables, eggs, fish, poultry and gratin dishes. The recipe that follows is considered traditional.

Sauce Béchamel

5 Tbsp clarified butter	2 Tbsp onion, chopped
2 oz (60 gr) very lean veal cut into small dice	1 small sprig thyme
	½ bay leaf
5 Tbsp flour	pinch of nutmeg
3 cups milk, brought to a boil before using	salt and white pepper

In a small skillet melt 1 Tbsp of the butter and in this cook the veal gently without allowing it to brown. (Note: the veal may be eliminated from the recipe. In that case the sauce is properly known as *Béchamel maigre*).

In a saucepan melt the remaining butter and to this add the flour and cook together over a low flame, stirring constantly with a wood spoon for 5 minutes. To this mixture (which is known as a "*roux*"), add the boiling milk, mix well, add the veal and remaining ingredients and simmer very gently for 45 minutes to 1 hour. Strain through a cloth. (Yields about 2 cups).

Hints about Béchamel Sauce

—When making Béchamel sauce, always use a heavy bottomed enameled stainless steel or Pyrex pot to prevent the sauce from burning on the bottom of the pot.

—When called for, an alternative is to add a whole onion into which 3 or 4 whole cloves have been stuck.

—Once the sauce is done, if it is lumpy force it through a fine sieve or process it in an electric blender and then simmer gently for 5 minutes. If the sauce is too thick, bring to a simmer and thin with milk, beating it a Tbsp at a time. If the sauce is too thin, blend ½ Tbsp of butter into a paste with 1 Tbsp of flour. Off the heat, beat this paste into the sauce with a wire whisk, and then boil for 1 minute, stirring constantly.

—If not using the sauce immediately, float a thin film of milk or melted butter on top, and set aside uncovered, or keep it hot by placing it in the top pot of a double boiler over hot but not boiling water.

Three Sauces based on Béchamel

Cream Sauce: This sauce is nothing more than Béchamel sauce enriched with sweet cream. After making the sauce as described above, bring it to a simmer and, a tablespoonful at a time, beat in ½ cup of sweet cream, simmering and mixing constantly until the sauce is at the consistency you want. Season to taste with salt, pepper and a few drops of lemon juice.

Sauce Mornay: Bring the Béchamel to a boil, remove from the heat and beat in ¼–½ cup of coarsely grated Gruyere cheese or a mixture of Gruyere and finely grated Parmesan cheese. Season to taste with salt, pepper, nutmeg and hot paprika. Remove from the heat and then stir in 1 Tbsp of butter.

Sauce Aurore: Bring the Béchamel to a simmer and then, a Tbsp at a time, stir in 2–6 Tbsp of tomato puree until you have achieved the color and flavor desired. Correct the seasoning to taste with salt and pepper. Remove from the flame and just before serving stir in 1–2 Tbsp of butter and finely chopped fresh parsley, basil or tarragon to taste.

François Vatel 1631–1671

A Man of Honor

No chef in culinary history has come to represent the supreme commitment of chefs to their vocation more than François Vatel. Born Fritz Karl Watel to a Swiss family of laborers, Vatel started his career as an apprentice with the Parisian pastry chef Evrard, and soon his services were much in demand due to his outstanding skills as an organizer of grand banquets.

Vatel presided over the kitchens of Nicolas Fouquet, who was Louise XIV's minister of finance for eight years, until he was implicated with fraud and was arrested in 1661. Fearing for his own fate, Vatel fled to England and came back to France only several years later to work for Louis II de Bourbon, Prince de Condé.

In the spring of 1671, the Prince de Condé was preparing a reception for King Louis XIV and an entourage of two hundred guests. Vatel, who was dedicated to raising the standards of the prince's chateau at Chantilly to those of Versailles, and who aspired to show his supremacy to the king's chef, La Varenne, took complete charge of the arrangements. He ensured that the lawns were mowed, the linens fresh and the curtains dusted. He arranged a grand spectacle of fireworks, prepared the menus, ordered the food, supervised its cooking, tasted the sauces, and carved the roasts.

The king arrived in the late afternoon of April 23rd, and went hunting in the evening with his party. Afterwards he supped on turtle soup, creamed chicken, fried trout and roast pheasant in the daffodil garden. Unfortunately, the cloudy weather crippled the fireworks spectacle, and, because seventy-five guests more than anticipated had arrived, there were not enough pheasants for several of the tables. Vatel felt that his honor had been stained, but the prince, on noting his chef's agitation, went out of his way to praise the meal.

The next day, a Friday, Vatel was expecting a large shipment of fish for the day's meals. When only a few baskets arrived, he became distraught, his mind reeling with visions of the king and his court sitting

down to empty plates. "The shame is too much to bear," he wrote—and stabbed himself eight times. Shortly after his body was found, the rest of the fish arrived.

The meal went ahead as planned, featuring anchovies Sevigné, melon with Parma ham, lobster quenelles with shrimp sauce, leg of lamb, Vatel duck in Madeira wine and for dessert—strawberry bombe. One dish, a fillet of sole, had been omitted from the menu as homage to the chef. Madame de Sevigné, whose account of the affair is often mentioned, was not in fact present at the dinner but heard about it from a friend. To her daughter she wrote: "the man protected his honor, of that one can be certain...the incident did, of course, spoil the party somewhat."

Vatel's act started what could almost be called a tradition among French chefs. During the height of the turmoil of the French Revolution, for example, Antoine Brossard, chef to the financier Laurent Grimod de la Reynière, found that he could not locate any Nantes ducklings to prepare for dinner. Brossard prepared a light dinner for his employer, wrote a long note of apology, and then hung himself in his kitchen.

The following recipes were both devised by Vatel.

Gigot d'Agneau à la Vatel
Leg of Lamb à la Vatel

This is a country-style dish devised by Vatel about two years before his death. The meat should be tender enough to eat with a spoon.

1 leg of lamb, about 5½ lb (2½ kilos), trimmed and tied	1 cup beef or chicken stock
6 cloves garlic, cut into slivers	1 Tbsp tomato paste
¼ cup butter	1 bouquet garni made by tying together 3 sprigs of parsley, 2 sprigs of thyme and 1 bay leaf
3 carrots, sliced	
3 medium onions, sliced	
1 cup dry white wine	salt and pepper to taste

With a sharp knife make small slits in the meat and into each slit insert a garlic sliver.

Melt the butter in a heavy saucepan or flameproof casserole dish.

Add the carrots and onions, sauté gently for several minutes and in this brown the meat on all sides. Add the wine, cook for 1–2 minutes and then add the stock and tomato paste, stirring in well. Season to taste with salt and pepper and add the bouquet garni.

Cover the casserole dish and roast the lamb in an oven that has been preheated to low for 6–7 hours. After cooking, very gently remove the meat to a serving platter. Strain the cooking liquids and pour over the meat. (Serves 6).

Caneton à la Madeira
Duckling with Madeira Sauce

1 duckling, about 5 lb (2¼ kilo), quartered
2 Tbsp olive oil
1 medium onion, chopped
2 Tbsp flour
½ cup red wine
½ cup beef or chicken stock
1 bouquet garni made by tying together 3 sprigs parsley, 2 sprigs thyme and 1 bay leaf

2 shallots, chopped
1 clove garlic, crushed
salt and pepper to taste
3 oz (85 gr) mushrooms, sliced thinly
¼ cup Madeira wine
1 cup toasted bread croutons
chopped parsley for garnish

In a large heavy skillet heat the oil and in this sauté the duckling quarters. Turn skin side down and continue cooking until the skin is well browned and the fat has been rendered. Remove the duckling pieces and set aside to keep warm.

Discard all but 2 Tbsp of the fat and into this stir the onion and sauté until lightly browned. Add the flour and continue cooking, stirring constantly over a medium flame until browned. Whisk in the wine, stock, bouquet garni, shallots, garlic, salt and pepper. Return the duck to the skillet, cover and simmer until the duck is tender when pierced with a fork (about 30 minutes). Add more stock during cooking if the sauce becomes thick.

Add the mushrooms and Madeira and simmer until the mushrooms are tender (3–4 minutes). The sauce should be thick enough to coat the back of a spoon. Remove the duckling pieces to a serving platter and if the sauce is too thick add stock; if too thin boil to reduce further.

Discard the bouquet garni and correct the seasoning. Surround the duckling pieces with the croutons and over this spoon the mushrooms and sauce. If ample sauce remains, serve in a gravy boat. Garnish with the parsley immediately before serving. (Serves 4).

Samuel Pepys, 1633–1703

Delicious Entries

S amuel Pepys, the famous English diarist, is remembered not so much for his recounting of historical events such as the coronation of Charles II or the great fire of London but for his daily accounts of his social and domestic life, including his numerous meals and amorous affairs. A native of London, in 1654 Pepys entered the service of Edward Montague, the future Earl of Sandwich and First Lord of the Admiralty, and shortly afterwards joined the civil service as a clerk with the Navy Board. In 1660 he started his diary and for almost ten years wrote his vivid daily impressions of seventeenth century London, at that time a city of half a million people with an abundance of taverns, shops and entertainment outlets.

Due to a decline in his eyesight, Pepys abandoned the diary in 1669. Nevertheless, he continued his active life, and served as Secretary for the Admiralty, a Member of Parliament and president of the Royal Society. Upon his death, fellow diarist John Evelyn wrote: "This day died Mr. Sam Pepys, a very worthy, industrious, and curious person."

In addition to enjoying many dinners at his own home and at the lodgings of his friends, Pepys was a frequent guest at the best of the London taverns of his time—the Swan, the Sun, the Dog and the Leg being among his favorites. In a dinner he had with the Earl of Sandwich, his employer, on 26 January 1660, they ate "a dish of marrow bones; a leg of mutton; a loin of veal; a dish of fowl, three pullets, and two dozen of larks all in a dish; a great tart, a neat's tongue, a dish of anchovies; a dish of prawns and cheese." A year later, on 1 January 1661, when entertaining his father, brother and uncle, he gave them "a barrel of oysters, a dish of neat's tongue and a dish of anchovies, wine of all sorts, and Northdown ale."

One of Pepys' favorite's foods was oysters. They are mentioned sixty-eight times in his diary. In an entry on 21 April 1660 Pepys writes: "In the afternoon the Captain would by all means have me up to his cabin, and there treated me huge nobly, giving me a barrel of pickled oysters, and opened another for me, and a bottle of wine, which was a very great favor." He also savored mince pies, and on 6 January 1662, celebrating the wedding anniversary of Sir W. Penn, he and his friends had a feast of "chine of beef and other good cheer, eighteen mince pies in a dish, the number of the years that he hath been married." In seventeenth century England, a standard recipe of mince pie would include a rabbit, a pigeon, a partridge, a hare, a pheasant, a capon, the livers of all these animals, as well as eggs, pickled mushrooms, dried fruit and spices.

Pepys was also fond of venison pasty, and in an entry from 1 September 1660 he writes, "we dined at the Bullhead upon the best venison pasty that ever I eat of in my life, and with one dish more, it was the best dinner I ever was at." Following is a modernized version of this dish.

Venison Pasty

FOR THE PASTRY:
1 cup flour, sifted
½ tsp salt
¼ cup vegetable shortening
3 Tbsp butter
2 eggs beaten together lightly
     with 1 tsp water

FOR THE FILLING:

1 lb (450 gr) venison meat, chopped finely

¼ lb (115 gr) fatty bacon, diced

2 medium onions, chopped finely

2 medium potatoes, peeled and cut into small cubes

1 small sweet potato, peeled and cut into small cubes

1 Tbsp parsley, chopped coarsely

salt and pepper to taste

peach or mango chutney for serving

Prepare the pastry dough: Combine the flour and salt and resift. Combine the vegetable shortening and butter and then cut half of this mixture into the flour, working it in gently with the tips of the fingers until it has the texture of cornmeal. Cut in the remaining shortening and continue working with the fingertips until the pastry is in pea-size bits.

Sprinkle the dough with 2½ Tbsp water and blend the water lightly into the dough. If necessary add more water—just enough to bind the ingredients.

Note: If covered with plastic wrap and refrigerated, the pastry dough can be prepared up to 24 hours in advance. Do not freeze, because the pastry tends to become dry.

Prepare the filling by combining all of the ingredients in a mixing bowl, mixing well by hand.

Sprinkle a large working surface with flour and on this roll out the pastry to a large rectangle. Spread the filling in a sausage like shape in the center of the dough. Brush the uncovered edges of the dough with the beaten eggs. Fold over the ends of the dough, fold the sides over the filling and seal by pinching the ends together. Brush again with the beaten egg mixture.

Transfer the roll to an oven that has been preheated to medium and bake until the pastry begins to brown. Cover lightly with aluminum foil and cook 20–30 minutes longer. About 3 minutes before the cooking is done remove and discard the aluminum foil. Remove from the oven, and let cool. Serve warm, ideally accompanied by peach or mango chutney. (Serves 4–6).

Pickled Oysters

48 oysters, shucked, with the
    liquids reserved

FOR THE MARINADE:

1 tsp each, allspice, cloves and
    mace, all ground
1 tsp sugar
½ tsp each cinnamon and salt

6 whole peppercorns
3 onions, peeled and halved
1 cup white wine vinegar
2 Tbsp Sherry wine

In a moderate-sized saucepan combine all of the marinade ingredients. Bring to a boil, reduce the heat and simmer for 3 minutes. Let cool completely, cover, and then refrigerate until well chilled. Add the oysters and their liquids. Mix well, cover and marinate 8–12 hours.

Return the mixture to the heat and bring to the boil. Let boil for 1 minute and then remove from the flame, let cool and refrigerate until well chilled. To serve, remove the oysters with a slotted spoon. Serve with toasted bread and butter. (Serves 8 as a first course).

Madame de Maintenon, 1635–1719
Bel Esprit

Francoise d'Aubigné was a penniless sixteen-year-old orphan of genteel birth when she married the celebrated burlesque writer Paul Scarron in 1652. Eight years later she was a young widow who was accepted in the best salons of Paris, where she was referred to as the charming unfortunate, *la charmante malheureuse*. In 1670 she undertook the education of the bastard children of King Louis XIV and his mistress Madame de Montespan.

When the king declared the children legitimate in 1674, Francoise moved to live with them in court. The king considered her to be a *bel esprit*, a woman of wit and intellect. After a short time he gave her an allowance generous enough that she could buy the Maintenon estate, and the following year she was introduced at court as Madame de Maintenon. In 1684, a few months after the queen's death, the king married her secretly, and for the rest of his life she was his closest confidant.

Madame de Maintenon was to play a prominent role in politics for the next thirty years, her austere manner and religious devotion influencing the entire court. The king used to have his cabinet meetings in her rooms; she received diplomats, princes and generals, and engaged

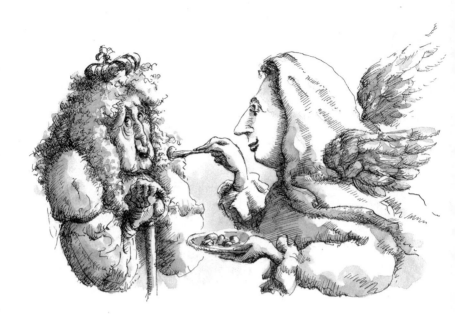

herself in charitable works. On his deathbed, the king said of her: "She helped me in everything, especially in saving my soul."

Maintenon is remembered as well as the founder of Saint-Cyr, an elite school for impoverished noble girls. Some speculate that the term *cordon bleu* originated in this school, as the students wore a blue sash in their final year of studies, during which they were required to master the skills of cookery. The Marquise, her own tastes refined and delicate, did not approve of the vulgar dining habits of the king, and once observed that "if I ate half as much as he did, I would be dead within a week."

Like many of the members of royalty of her time, Maintenon enjoyed dabbling in the kitchen. Whether she or La Varenne invented the many dishes that today carry her name is not known, but many of them are considered among the finest dishes of French cookery. The first recipe that follows was one of Maintenon's personal favorites, and the second was devised for the king in his old age when, dyspeptic and toothless, he could no longer digest the huge roasts he had earlier adored.

Pommes de Terres Farci à la Maintenon
Stuffed Potatoes à la Maintenon

4 very large potatoes, unpeeled
    and very well cleaned
2 Tbsp butter, melted, and ¼
    cup butter
¼ lb (115 gr) onions, chopped
1 cup Béchamel sauce (see
    p. 67)
¼ tsp ground nutmeg

¼ cup sweet cream
½ cup cooked chicken breast,
    chopped
¼ cup smoked or pickled
    tongue, chopped
¼ cup mushrooms, chopped
¼ cup Parmesan cheese, grated
salt and pepper to taste

Brush the potatoes with the melted butter, sprinkle with salt and bake in a hot oven. After 20 minutes, pierce the skin of each potato once with the tines of a fork. Bake until the potatoes are soft and flaky inside (40–60 minutes, depending on the size of the potatoes).

While the potatoes are baking, plunge the onions into boiling water and let boil for 5–6 minutes. Drain. In a skillet melt 2 Tbsp of the butter and in this sauté the onions until they are translucent. Over a low flame, stirring constantly, add the Béchamel sauce, and season with salt, pepper and nutmeg. Press the mixture through a strainer, reheat and add the sweet cream and 2 more Tbsp of the butter. Mix together well and then mix in the chicken, tongue, and mushrooms and correct the seasoning with salt and pepper to taste.

When the potatoes are done, scoop out ⅔ of the pulp. Rub the pulp through a sieve and add it to the chicken mixture. With this mixture refill the potato skins. Sprinkle with the Parmesan cheese and place under a hot grill just until the top is nicely browned. Serve piping hot. (Serves 4).

Côtelettes de Mouton à la Maintenon
Mutton Cutlets à la Maintenon

8 mutton cutlets, bone intact,
   cut 1½″ (4 cm) thick
3 Tbsp butter
1½ Tbsp olive oil
1 Tbsp onion, chopped
½ cup champignon
   mushrooms, chopped
   coarsely

2 Tbsp flour
3 Tbsp beef stock
1 tsp chopped parsley
salt and cayenne pepper to
   taste
Espagnole sauce for serving
   (see p. 94)

In a heavy skillet heat together the olive oil and half of the butter and in this sauté the onion until just beginning to brown. Add the mushrooms and continue to sauté for 5 minutes longer. Add the remaining butter, stir until melted and then add the flour, beef stock, parsley and salt and cayenne pepper to taste. Cook over a low flame, stirring constantly until the mixture is smooth throughout.

Split each cutlet by cutting in the center clear to the bone, spread the cutlets and in the space between the two halves, pack the onion and mushroom mixture, pressing together lightly. Gently transfer the cutlets to a heavy skillet and fry over a medium-high flame until done on both sides, turning carefully just once (about 10 minutes cooking time in all). With a large spatula transfer the cutlets to individual serving plates and serve immediately with Espagnole sauce. (Serves 4).

King Louis XIV, 1638–1715

Absolutely Divine

L ouis XIV, known as *le Roi Soleil*, ate with his mouth open, consumed outrageous quantities of food and never stopped talking during his meals. Despite these failings, during his long reign of fifty-three years, France became the most prominent country in Europe, and many attribute the supremacy of French gastronomy to him.

The man who built Versailles, and whose motto was *l'état c'est moi* entertained magnificently. In 1656 Louis served a banquet that consisted of sixteen hot hors d'œuvres, fourteen different pâtés, ten soups, twelve fish dishes, sixteen meat dishes, sixteen vegetable dishes, thirty-two salads, twelve game pies and twenty-four different cakes. It is said, in mitigation, that he himself partook of only sixty of the various offerings. On another occasion, the queen's sister reported that in one sitting, the king ate "four soups, a pheasant, a partridge, a plate of salad, sliced mutton with garlic, two lumps of ham, a plate of pastries, fruits and preserves."

Louis insisted on eating with his fingers and always wore a hat at the dinner table. Since he had the good manners to doff his hat to the ladies of the court, the brim of the royal hat was always thoroughly coated with the grease of whatever he had been eating. It is known that he incapacitated himself with food on his wedding night, and Saint-Simon, the chronicler of the court, reports in his memoirs that the autopsy carried out after the king's death revealed a royal stomach twice the size of that of an ordinary man.

A notorious gourmand, Louis saw fine dining as a way to glorify himself, but at the same time as a means to govern, to create the cultural hegemony needed to substantiate his absolute monarchy. Saint-Simon paid tribute to the king for

encouraging
service in the French manner,
with all the dishes served at once and guests placed around the table according to a meticulous plan. It was during Louis's reign, in the seventeenth century, that La Varenne published the first important cookbook, *Le Cuisinier Français*, Dom Pérignon invented the Champagne

method of wine production, coffee was introduced to Europe, the croissant was born, and French chefs abandoned the excessive use of spices in favor of shallots and truffles. Many new vegetables and fruits arrived in France from the colonies—although it is said that when Louis ate a pineapple for the first time he took such a giant bite that he cut his lips and consequently outlawed the fruit.

The two dishes that follow are those most often found on modern tables, and were devised in Louis's memory some two hundred and fifty years after the king and his stomach were laid to rest. Some claim that these dishes were first made in Davenport Hotel in Spokane, Washington, but it is more probable that they were created at San Francisco's St. Francis Hotel by chef Victor Hirtzler.

Crab Louis

1 cup mayonnaise
½ cup sweet cream
½ cup chili sauce
¼ cup green pepper, chopped
the white parts of 6 spring
    onions, chopped
½ tsp Worcestershire sauce

4 whole lettuce leaves
1 cup lettuce leaves, shredded
2 cups cooked crab meat
2 Tbsp chives or the green part
    of spring onions, chopped
salt and pepper to taste

In a small mixing bowl combine the mayonnaise, cream, chili sauce, green pepper, spring onions and Worcestershire sauce. Mix well and then add salt and pepper to taste.

In each of 4 serving glasses or on small plates lay a lettuce leaf. Over this distribute the shredded lettuce and onto this spoon the crab meat. Over the crab distribute the mayonnaise dressing and then sprinkle the chopped chives over the dish. May be served immediately or chilled for no more than 1 hour before serving. (Serves 4 as a first course).

Curried Shrimps Louis

1¾ lb (800 gr) shrimps, in their shells
juice of 1 lime
2 Tbsp each olive oil
1 medium onion, chopped coarsely
2 medium tomatoes, peeled and chopped

2 Tbsp chives or the green part of spring onions, chopped
2 Tbsp curry powder
1½ cups chicken or fish stock
2 Tbsp butter
2 Tbsp flour
2 whole pineapples

In a saucepan bring a large amount of lightly salted water to a rolling boil and into this plunge the shrimp. Maintain the boil and cook until the shrimp are pink. Drain, run under cold water and peel the shrimps. Rinse well, pour over the lime juice, let stand for 5 minutes and drain again.

In a heavy skillet, heat the oil and in this sauté the onion, the tomatoes and half the chives (or green onions), together with the curry powder. Sauté for 5 minutes, taking care not to brown. Add the stock and shrimp, and simmer over the lowest possible flame for 10 minutes. Remove from the flame.

Blend together the butter and flour and add this slowly to the shrimp mixture. Return to a low flame and, stirring constantly, cook until the mixture is completely smooth (3–4 minutes longer). Remove from the flame.

In a large saucepan bring to the boil a large amount of water and into this plunge the pineapples for 3–4 minutes. Drain and halve the pineapples lengthwise, leaving the leaves intact. Hollow out most of the flesh, fill the hollows with the shrimp mixture and place under a hot grill for 3–4 minutes. Remove from the grill, sprinkle over the remaining chives and serve hot. (Serves 4 as a first course or luncheon dish).

The Duchess of Berry, 1695–1719
A Saucy Lady

The Duchesse de Berry, Marie Louise Elisabeth d'Orleans, a granddaughter of Louis XIV, has often been described as "The French Messalina." It was rumored that she was mad, and there is enough evidence to show that she was both bulimic and alcoholic. Her father, the Duc d'Orleans, was so obsessed with her that their relationship became the subject of gossip in all the salons of Paris. Her grandmother, the Princess Palatine, wrote of her: "She never leaves her room before noon and spends her mornings in eating all kinds of delicacies. At two o'clock she sits down to an elaborate dinner.... At ten she has a heavy supper, and retires to bed between one and two in the morning. She likes very strong brandy."

At fifteen she was married to the weak and boorish Duc de Berry, whom she despised, and she soon took lovers. When her husband threatened to have her shut up in a convent, she laughed in his face. Violent scenes would follow, and in one of them, as Saint-Simon, the chronicler of the court reported, the duchess "received a kick." She was known to get drunk often and to faint in the middle of dinner. On occasion she would have bouts of vomiting after gorging herself, as in one recorded case when she had attended the theatre, where she continually stuffed herself for two hours with caramelized peaches, chestnuts, gooseberries and dried cherries.

Subsequent to the death of her husband in 1714, and the death of the king in the following year, her father became Regent of France, and her conduct became even more outrageous. She invited her father to dine with her lovers at her rooms at the Luxembourg Palace, and went to the Palais-Royal to sup with his friends and mistresses, suppers that often evolved into fully-fledged orgies.

In 1718 she gave a ball at the Luxembourg Palace in honor of her aunt, the Duchess of Lorraine, and at one meal served 132 hors-d'œuvres, 32 soups, 60 entrées, 130 hot entremets, 60 cold entremets, 72 *plats ronds*, 82 pigeons, 370 partridges and pheasants, and 126 sweetbreads. The dessert consisted of 100 baskets of fresh fruit, 94 baskets of dried fruit, 50 dishes of fruits glacées and 106 compotes. She herself ate enormous amounts of food daily, and by the time of her death due to a bad cold, just short of her twenty-fourth birthday, she was extremely fat.

Filets de Lapereau Berry
Fillets of Rabbit à la Berry

Fillets of 6–8 young rabbits
2 Tbsp olive oil
2 Tbsp butter
6 oz (180 gr) mushrooms, sliced
2 shallots, chopped
2 truffles, sliced thinly and cut into julienne strips
3 Tbsp brandy
3 Tbsp white wine

½ cup *demi-glace* sauce or Espagnole (see p. 94)
2 Tbsp tomato puree
2–3 Tbsp concentrated beef stock
4–5 leaves tarragon, chopped
3–4 sprigs parsley, chopped
salt and freshly ground pepper to taste

Cut the rabbit fillets into small noisettes and season to taste with salt and pepper. In a heavy skillet heat the oil and butter together and over a high flame quickly sauté the noisettes just until they begin to brown on both sides. Remove with a slotted spoon and set aside to keep warm.

To the skillet add the sliced mushrooms and sauté these for 2–3 minutes. Add the shallots, truffles, brandy and wine, bring to a boil and boil until reduced by about ⅓. Add the *demi-glace* or Espagnole sauce, tomato sauce, concentrated meat stock, tarragon and parsley, return to the boil for several seconds and then return the noisettes to the sauce just to heat them through. Serve immediately. (Serves 4).

Pommes de Terre Duchesse
Duchess Potatoes

1½ lb (675 gr) potatoes peeled
    and cut into equal-sized
    pieces
½ cup butter
3 egg yolks
pinch of nutmeg
salt and white pepper to taste

In a large saucepan with lightly salted water to cover bring the potatoes to a boil. Cover and simmer until the potatoes are quite soft (about 20 minutes). Drain the potatoes and return them to the saucepan, cooking on a very low flame, shaking occasionally, until dry.

Press the potatoes through a sieve and return to the saucepan. Beat in the butter, salt, pepper and nutmeg and continue beating, over a very low flame, until the mixture is light and fluffy. Remove from the flame and beat in the egg yolks. Correct the seasoning with salt and pepper to taste.

Vincent de La Chapelle, 1698–1772
Modern Times

Remembered today mainly as the inventor of Sauce Espagnole, Vincent de La Chapelle was also the author of one of the most influential cookbooks in eighteen century Europe, *The Modern Cook*. The book was first published in London in 1733, where La Chapelle served as chef to the Earl of Chesterfield, and then two year later was released in Paris under the title *Le Cuisinier Moderne*. In it La Chapelle presented his interpretation of *nouvelle cuisine*, a new kind of cookery that became popular in France in the first half of the eighteenth century as a reaction to the *ancienne cuisine* of Louis XIV.

The book contains recipes that are relatively simple and perfectly appropriate for the modern kitchen, including, for example, sole stuffed with herbs, anchovy fillets and capers poached in white wine, and mackerel with fennel and gooseberries. Although some argue that La Chapelle borrowed many of his recipes from his predecessor, François Massialot, who published a book on court cookery in 1692, his innovations are still valuable, as, for example in the recipe for *coulis*, where he uses a flour-based roux instead of the breadcrumbs that had traditionally been used up to that time in order to thicken sauces.

In addition to simplifying the intricate dishes of the *ancienne cuisine*, he also incorporated many elements from foreign cuisines, which have since become standard in French cuisine. In the preface to the English version of his book, La Chapelle writes: "A cook of genius will invent new delicacies to please the palates of those for whom he is to labour; his art, like all others, being subject to change; for should the table of a great man be served in the taste that prevailed twenty years ago, it would not please the guests, how strictly soever he might conform to the rules laid down at that time."

La Chapelle, of Huguenot extraction, spent some years in exile, first in England as chef to Lord Chesterfield, and then in the Netherlands as the cook of William IV, Prince of Orange. He also worked in Germany, Portugal and in the East Indies, before returning to France to serve as chief cook in the court of Louis XV, where he dedicated several dishes to Queen Marie Leszczyńska, among them the famous *bouchées à la reine.* The first two of the recipes that follow are from *The Modern Cook,* and the third is a modern adaptation of Sauce Espagnole.

To make a Potage for one or two Persons

Take four Handfuls of Pot-herbs, pick'd, wash'd and cut small, two or three Onions cut small likewise, three or four Leeks, Half an Ounce of fresh Butter or Bacon, four Spoonfuls either of fine Flour, pounded Rice, Oatmeal, or peel'd Barley, a Dram of Salt, and a little Pepper; boil the whole in three Quarts of Water, which must be reduced to a Pint and a Half, and kept for use. You may make at the same time Potage enough for three or four days.

A moistening and cooling Broth with Herbs

Take some Leaves of Sorrel, Lettuce, Purslane, and Chervil, two large handfuls of each, pick, wash and cut them all small, let them boil with a Crust of Bread and two Drams of fresh Butter in two Pints of Water, which when half boiled away it should be taken off and strained through a Sieve.

Sauce Espagnole

The most classic and, some say, the most magnificent of all brown sauces, Espagnole can be used on its own with many cuts of meat, or may serve as the basis for making *demi-glace* and many other brown sauces.

1 Tbsp butter
1 medium carrot, diced
1 medium onion, diced
2 inner ribs of celery, diced
1 Tbsp uncooked bacon,
　　minced
½ bay leaf, crushed
1 sprig thyme
½ tsp Madeira wine

¼ cup beef drippings
¼ cup flour
8 black peppercorns
¼ cup parsley, chopped
　　coarsely
2 medium-large tomatoes,
　　peeled and chopped
　　coarsely
4 cups beef stock

In a skillet melt the butter and in this sauté the diced vegetables, bacon, bay leaf and thyme until the vegetables are soft. Add the Madeira and mix gently, deglazing the pan.

In a heavy saucepan melt the beef drippings and to this add the vegetable mixture. Cook until the vegetables begin to brown and then add the flour. Stir until the flour is well browned. Add the peppercorns, tomatoes and parsley, mixing in well, and then add the beef stock. Simmer on a low to moderate flame until the sauce is reduced by about half (about 2½ hours). During the cooking, stir occasionally, skimming off the fat as it rises.

After the sauce has been reduced remove from the flame and strain. The finished sauce should be approximately the consistency of whipping cream. (Yields about 3 cups).

Marie Leszczyńska, 1703–1768

Holding Court

Many famous dishes are named *à la reine*, literally, in the style of the queen, but even the usually reliable *Larousse Gastronomique* often has difficulty identifying the specific queens who inspired each of the dishes. However, there are some that we know were dedicated to the docile Marie Leszczyńska, who, as her husband, King Louis XV, wrote of her, "was far more interested in what happened in her kitchens than in my bed."

Maria Karolina Zofia Felicja Leszczyńska was a daughter of the dethroned King Stanislaw I of Poland, who was living in exile in Alsace. She was chosen as the bride to Louis XV because Cardinal Fleury, the Prime Minister, thought that her modest lineage would prevent future conflicts between France and its allies. His hopes did not bear fruit, however—Leszczyńska's dynastic connections did involve France in a conflict over Poland that ultimately resulted in the annexation of Lorraine by France.

Leszczyńska was twenty-two and Louis only fifteen when they were married in 1725. The queen fulfilled her obligations and bore ten children, including an heir to the throne. During the first years of their marriage, Louis was devoted to his queen, but in 1733 he took a

mistress, and after the queen bore their tenth child in 1737, he never spoke to her again except when others were present. By 1745, Madame de Pompadour had become his official mistress, and as Louis preferred the company of his mistress to that of his wife, the queen was practically excluded from court.

She held her own court in her chambers, carrying out ceremonial duties and receiving many guests, among them Voltaire and the young Mozart. Leszczyńska, a devout Roman Catholic, attended mass twice a day, painted, embroidered, and played the guitar and harpsichord. In the evening she would dine with a small group of friends, enjoying the dishes that the chief cook of the court, Vincent de la Chapelle, devised for her—*poulet à la reine, filet braisé à la royale, consommé à la reine* and *bouchées à la reine.*

The Queen led a quiet life until her death at the age of sixty-five. She left behind three grandchildren who would be kings of France— Louis XVI who was guillotined during the French Revolution, and Louis XVIII and Charles X who became kings after the restoration of the monarchy in the nineteenth century.

Bouchées à la Reine

Bouchées (literally "a mouthful") are among the most classic of French hors d'œuvres. Although there is nothing easy about making this dish, the effort proves well worthwhile.

TO MAKE THE BOUCHÉES (PASTRY SHELLS):
Bouchées are always made with puff pastry that has been baked blind and filled with various mixtures. To prepare 10 4″ (10 cm) bouchées, roll puff pastry into a rectangle of about 7″ × 15″ (18 × 40 cm). With a 2″ or 3″ (5 or 7½ cm) hot fluted pastry cutter cut out ten circles. Using a 2″–2½″ (5–6 cm) pastry cutter make incisions in each circle that penetrate about ⅔ through the dough, taking care not to push the cutter all the way through. Refrigerate for about 1 hour and then bake in a medium oven just until the pastries have risen and are light goldenbrown in color. As soon as the shells are removed from the oven, release the inner circles and set aside, leaving a hollow ring of pastry. The hollow

shells are filled and the top halves of the smaller circles can be baked separately and used as tops for the shells.

TO PREPARE THE ALLEMANDE SAUCE:

3 cups chicken or veal stock	salt and pepper to taste
3 Tbsp butter	2 Tbsp sweet cream
3 Tbsp flour	1 Tbsp lemon juice
pinch of nutmeg	1 egg yolk

Prepare the sauce by bringing 2 cups of the chicken stock to a boil in a clean saucepan. In a heavy skillet melt 2 Tbsp of the butter and then whisk the flour and nutmeg into the butter and cook over a low flame until the mixture is foaming but not brown. Remove from the flame and let stand for 2–3 minutes before whisking in the hot stock Bring again to the boil, whisking continuously, and season very lightly with salt and pepper. Reduce the flame and simmer until the sauce has begun to thicken, skimming the surface occasionally and whisking every minute or two.

Add the remaining chicken stock into the mixture, blend well and reduce by cooking on a medium heat until the sauce is reduced to ⅔ of its original volume. Be careful not to let the mixture boil.

Mix the egg yolk with the cream.

Remove the sauce from the flame and add the egg yolk and cream mixture. Stir until the sauce is thickened. Immediately before using, stir in the lemon juice and remaining butter. (Yields about 1½ cups).

FOR THE FILLING:

½ lb (225 gr) chicken breast, cooked and cut into very small dice	1–2 whole truffles, grated or, if unavailable 1 tsp truffle paste
¼ lb (115 gr) champignon mushrooms, lightly sautéed in butter	about ½ cup Allemande sauce (see recipe above)

To prepare the dish gently mix together the filling ingredients with just enough of the Allemande sauce to bind. With this mixture fill the *bouchées*. Distribute the shells on a baking sheet together with the reserved top halves of the shells and transfer to a medium oven just until the *bouchées* are heated through (about 6–8 minutes). Cover each shell with its top and serve at once, ideally accompanied by a small green salad. (Serves 4–5 as a luncheon dish or first course).

Consommé à la Reine

9 cups chicken consommé
2¼ Tbsp chervil or, if unavailable, parsley, chopped
1 egg + 2 egg yolks, beaten together

6 Tbsp tapioca
1 large cooked breast of chicken, shredded coarsely, warm or at room temperature

First prepare the garnish: Bring 1 cup of the consommé to the boil and remove from the flame. Sprinkle in ¼ Tbsp of the chervil and let stand for 10–12 minutes, and then slowly blend the eggs into the mixture. Strain, skim and pour into a buttered mold. Place in a double boiler, covered, over hot water, until firm. Let cool, refrigerate and when completely cold turn out of the mold and cut into ½″ (1 cm) dice. (This classic preparation is known as a *royale*).

Make the soup: Bring the remaining consommé to the boil and sprinkle in the tapioca. Let boil for 18 minutes, stirring occasionally, and then strain through muslin or a fine sieve. Garnish with the *royale*, shredded chicken and remaining chervil. (Serves 6).

Note: To make the dish known as Consommé Lucullus, replace the chervil with 6–8 mint leaves and 2 tsp chives, both chopped finely.

Cœurs d'Artichaut à la Reine
Hearts of Artichoke à la Reine

8 large artichoke hearts,
    cooked, at room
    temperature
3 Tbsp butter
3 Tbsp onion, chopped

1 lb (450 gr) mushrooms,
    chopped
3 Tbsp sweet cream
salt and black pepper to taste

In a skillet, melt the butter, and in this sauté the onions and mushrooms until they have browned. To these add the sweet cream and the salt and pepper and heat through. Fill the artichoke hearts with this mixture and place in a hot oven for 5 minutes. Serve hot. (Serves 4 as a first course).

Charles de Rohan, 1715–1787

Esprit de Corps

C harles de Rohan, Prince de Soubise and general of the armies of France during the reign of King Louis X V, knew greater success in the kitchen than on the battlefield. In a career that lasted more than forty years, he never won a single battle. It is estimated that under his command sixteen thousand soldiers and officers died in combat, and that he lost more than eight hundred artillery pieces, two thousand six hundred horses, two hundred and forty donkeys and six camels to the enemy.

Despite his failings, Soubise is considered a hero by most Frenchmen. When he went off to the battlefield he would go with a wagon train of kitchen and dining equipment and the very best of foods and wines. Equally important, he was always accompanied by his personal chef, Marin. On one occasion, when overrun by the Prussians at Rossbach, the general lost nearly six hundred of his troops—but earned the respect of all of France by saving his chef and his *batterie de cuisine*. On another occasion, after a five day retreat from a battle he had lost, he sent a messenger to the commanding general of the Prussian army and requested a twenty-four hour ceasefire so that his chef would have

time to cook several pheasants. The Prussian commander agreed, and the opposing generals dined together that night.

Soubise was the last male in his family, but his name lives on thanks to an onion mixture known as Soubise, which is used for garnish and in making more than thirty-five different sauces. Whether the original concoction was first made by Marin or by Constant, the head chef at the Soubise family chateau is not known. The prince also has a sauce named after him, and like the Soubise, this too is based on onions together with Béchamel sauce. Today, all dishes named *à la Soubise* are served or stuffed with onion Soubise, or served with Sauce Soubise.

Soubise

½ lb (225 gr) onions, chopped
½ cup butter
2 cups thick Béchamel sauce
(see p. 67)

Salt, white pepper and nutmeg
¼ cup sweet cream

Place the onions in a generous amount of boiling water and let boil for 5–6 minutes. Drain well. In a skillet heat ¼ cup of the butter and in this gently cook, but do not brown the onions. Add the Béchamel sauce, season with salt, pepper and nutmeg and simmer gently for several minutes, stirring often. Rub through a sieve, pressing with a wood spoon. Reheat the puree, add the remaining butter and the cream and mix thoroughly. If not using at once, dab the surface with butter and keep warm in a *bain-marie*. (Yields about 2½ cups).

Cœurs d'Artichauts Soubise
Hearts of Artichokes Soubise

12 artichoke hearts
juice of 1 lemon
¼ cup butter

2½ cups Soubise (see recipe
above)

Drop the artichoke hearts into 2½ cm. of boiling water to which the lemon juice has been added and simmer, covered, until the hearts are nearly tender (16–20 minutes). Drain well.

In a skillet melt the butter and in this cook the hearts until tender (an additional 4–6 minutes). Drain and fill the hearts with the soubise. Serve hot as a vegetable or as a garnish. (Serves 6).

Pommes de Terre Soubise
Potatoes Soubise

6 large potatoes, in their jackets, washed and scrubbed
2 Tbsp butter, melted
salt and pepper

1 recipe Soubise (see previous page)
3 Tbsp butter
breadcrumbs as required

Brush the potatoes with the melted butter and sprinkle lightly with salt. In a very hot oven bake the potatoes for 20 minutes and then quickly prick the skin once with the tip of a fork and continue to bake until the potatoes are nicely done. Cut open the top of the potatoes and scoop out ⅔ of the pulp. Rub the pulp through a sieve and mix with the onion soubise. Season well with salt and pepper and add the remaining butter, mixing in well. Fill the potatoes with this mixture. Sprinkle over with the breadcrumbs and place under a hot grill until they begin to brown. Serve piping hot. (Serves 6).

Sauce Soubise

This sauce is traditionally served with grilled meats.

1 lb (450 gr) onions, chopped
⅔ cup butter
pinch each of salt, white pepper and nutmeg

2 cups Béchamel sauce (see p. 67)
2–3 Tbsp sweet cream

Place the onions in a generous amount of boiling water and blanch for 5–6 minutes. Drain well. Put the onions in a low, oven-proof casserole dish and dab with ¼ cup of the butter. Sprinkle over the salt, pepper and nutmeg and mix well, melting the butter and coating the onions. Cook in an oven that has been preheated to low for 30 minutes, taking care not to brown the onions. When the onions are cooked add the Béchamel sauce, stirring well, and return to the oven. Cook, covered, for 30 minutes longer and then rub through a sieve. Add the remaining butter and the sweet cream and blend together thoroughly. (Yields about 2½ cups).

Madame de Pompadour, 1721–1764
From the Prone Position

Jeanne-Antoinette Poisson, Madame de Pompadour, was an ambitious woman. Many say that as the official mistress of King Louis xv from 1745 until her death in 1764, she ruled France from the prone position. In one of their biting and sarcastic essays written the following century, Edmond and Jules Goncourt said that "Pompadour was the governing principle, the reason that directed, the voice that commanded. Nothing escaped her and she held everything, even the king of France, in her power."

Pompadour's influence was felt everywhere. She organized suppers and theater performances and endowed the court with a sense of extravagance. She commissioned philosophers and artists such as Voltaire and the painter François Boucher, encouraged the manufacture of porcelain and decorated the palace of Versailles in the Rococo style. She convinced the king to enter into an alliance with Austria, a pact that led to the disastrous Seven Years War; enticed him into elevating her cousin to Bishop of Paris; insisted that he promote a twenty-three-year-old officer to the rank of general; and cajoled him into passing a law forbidding the export of Burgundy wines to England. She convinced the king to support the writing of an encyclopedia which would be compiled by two of her brothers; induced him to open a new university in Grenoble, the rector of which would be her uncle; and she even redesigned the gardens at Versailles.

Precisely why Pompadour had such a powerful influence on the king is something of a mystery. Described by Louis' wife, Queen Marie Leszczyńska, as "ordinary, almost common in appearance, and possessed of a vulgar manner of speech," it is also known that Pompadour was sexually frigid. Hoping to stimulate her libido, she took on a diet of celery, truffles, and vanilla that harmed her health. When her friend, the Duchesse de Brancas, expressed concern, the royal mistress burst into tears and confessed that she had been terrified of not pleasing the king, who was known to have a very healthy sexual appetite. Indeed, Louis did tire of his mistress, and after a mere five years deserted her bed for better opportunities. Pompadour herself is known to have procured young girls for the king's bed while maintaining her status as his official mistress and confidante for the rest of her life. In a letter to his brother Louis wrote, "While it is true that I govern France, it is Pompadour who governs me."

Pompadour reigned over Versailles and her own chateau in Bellevue with an iron hand; not only the court but the kitchens as well. Members of royal households had an enormous desire to have dishes named after them, and Pompadour was powerful enough that more than fifty dishes, many of which are still popular, were dedicated to her. She also enjoyed dabbling in the kitchen and at her chateau in Bellevue she and her chefs devised a wide assortment of dishes, including the two that follow, which were especially devised for the pleasure of the king.

Filets de Sole à la Pompadour
Fillets of Sole à la Pompadour

12 fillets of sole
3 lb (1¼ kilos) shrimp, boiled
    and peeled
½ cup butter

2 cups chicken stock
½ cup dry white wine
salt and pepper to taste

With a mortar and pestle or in a blender, combine ⅓ of the shrimps with the butter, blending together thoroughly and then putting through a fine sieve. Transfer the mixture to a saucepan, heat through, and then remove from the flame until ready for further use.

In a large clean saucepan combine the chicken stock and wine and bring to a boil. Reduce to a bare simmer and in these liquids poach the sole fillets until they are just done (5–6 minutes). Gently remove the sole fillets to a preheated serving platter and set aside to keep warm.

Pour off all but 1 cup of the liquid in the saucepan and bring again to the boil, boiling until only ¼ cup of liquid remains. To this add the butter and shrimp mixture and, stirring constantly, heat through. Correct the seasoning of this sauce with salt and pepper to taste.

To serve, place the remaining shrimp around the sole fillets, spoon over a bit of the sauce and serve the remaining sauce separately. (Serves 6).

Abricots à la Pompadour
Apricots à la Pompadour

12 apricots, halved and pitted
2 cups milk, boiled with 2 tsp
    vanilla extract
1 heaping cup flour, sifted
3½ cups sugar
2 Tbsp kirsch liqueur
2 Tbsp butter

6 egg yolks
2 whole eggs
pinch of salt
3 stale brioches or croissants,
    sliced
breadcrumbs as required
oil or fat for deep frying

In a saucepan combine the milk, flour, kirsch, butter, egg yolks, whole eggs, salt and ½ cup of the sugar, mixing well. Bring the mixture to the boil and let boil for 2–3 minutes, stirring constantly. Pour this custard mixture into a ceramic bowl and stir periodically until cool.

In a separate saucepan, combine the remaining sugar with 2 cups of water. Bring to the boil, stirring, reduce the flame and in this syrup gently cook the apricot halves. Drain well.

Fill decorative skewers by threading on, alternately, brioche slices and apricot halves. Dip the skewers in the custard and then roll in the bread crumbs, coating well.

Heat the deep oil to the point of smoking and fry the skewered apricots until nicely browned. Drain, sprinkle over with the remaining sugar and serve hot as a dessert. (Serves 6–8).

Note: This recipe may also be made using peaches.

Antoine-Auguste Parmentier, 1737–1813

The Potato Man

Firrst brought to Spain from the New World around 1570, potatoes were considered poisonous by most Europeans and were treated with mistrust. So afraid were ordinary folk of these tubers, that when Sir Walter Raleigh decided to cultivate them in Ireland, his neighbors threatened to burn his house down. In 1630, fearing that the new tubers caused leprosy, the parliaments of Burgundy and Besançon in France passed laws that forbade their cultivation.

It took two hundred years and the efforts of pharmacist Antoine-Auguste Parmentier to rehabilitate the potato. As a prisoner of war in Prussia during the Seven Years War, Parmentier had survived for nearly two years on potatoes. On his return to France in 1763 he proposed to use the potato as nourishment for dysenteric patients, and in 1772 the Paris Faculty of Medicine declared potatoes edible. Still, resistance continued. Parmantier wrote a series of pamphlets praising potatoes and hosting dinners at which potato dishes featured, but it was not until he presented King Louis XVI with a bouquet of potato flowers and convinced the monarch to taste them that the potato became a culinary passion for royal families.

Even then, however, the common people remained leery.

Parmentier decided that the way to convince the masses was to arouse their cupidity. The king had given him several large fields near Paris in which to raise his potatoes. Parmentier arranged for soldiers to closely guard the fields during the day. At night, however, they were left unguarded. Human nature took over, and by the beginning of the revolution several years later, the potato had become France's most popular food. During the siege of Paris in 1795, potatoes were grown even in the Tuileries Gardens.

Throughout Europe, people became hard pressed to find enough superlatives for the potato. In London, Dr. William Salmon, a quack-doctor and writer, claimed that potatoes stopped "fluxes of the bowel and could cure tuberculosis and rabies." He went on to state that eating potatoes would "increase seed and provoke lust, causing fruitfulness in both sexes."

As to French fries, entitled by Curnonsky "the most spiritual creations of Parisian genius", they were probably first consumed under the bridges of Paris during the French Revolution, and were known as *pommes Pont-Neuf.*

Potage Parmentier

¾ cup sweet cream
1 lb (450 gr) potatoes, peeled and quartered
½ lb (225 gr) leeks, trimmed, well rinsed and cut into julienne strips

salt and freshly ground black pepper
3 Tbsp chopped fresh tarragon or chervil, for garnish

Combine the potatoes, leeks and 1 quart (1 liter) of water in a large saucepan. Bring to a boil over a high heat and then season with salt and pepper. Reduce the heat and simmer gently until the potatoes and leeks are very soft (about 35–40 minutes).

Puree the soup in a blender or food processor and then return to the saucepan. Stir in the sweet cream and cook over a low heat just until heated through. Adjust the seasoning to taste, sprinkle over the chopped herbs and serve immediately. (Serves 6–8).

Notes: (a) It is possible to use crème fraiche instead of sweet cream.
(b) During the winter this soup should be served hot. During the spring and summer months it may be served well chilled, ideally over a bowl of crushed ice.

Hachis Parmentier
Shepherd's Pie

1 lb (450 gr) ground beef (can substitute chicken)
1¾ lb (800 gr) potatoes, washed and peeled
6 slices fatty bacon, cut into julienne strips
1 red onion, chopped
2 cloves garlic, minced
2 leeks, trimmed and cut into rounds
2 stalks celery, sliced

2 Tbsp olive oil
3 Tbsp butter
1 bay leaf
1 Tbsp fresh thyme leaves
4 Tbsp parsley, chopped
8 Tbsp fresh breadcrumbs
4 Tbsp milk
3 Tbsp Gruyere cheese, grated
salt and pepper to taste

Boil the potatoes in lightly salted water until just tender. Drain and mash the potatoes coarsely.

In a large heavy skillet heat the olive oil together with 1 Tbsp of the butter. Separate the bacon into individual strips and add them to the skillet, tossing well. Add the onion, garlic, bay leaf and thyme and sauté for 3–4 minutes. Add the leek and celery, season to taste with salt and pepper, mix well and cover the skillet, letting cook over a low flame until the leeks are tender (8–10 minutes).

Add the beef to the skillet, stirring well. Add half of the parsley. Mix 3 Tbsp of the breadcrumbs with the milk and add this to the skillet, stirring well again. Raise the flame to moderately-high and sauté until the meat browns gently. Reduce the flame, cook for 12–15 minutes longer and add the remaining parsley 2–3 minutes before cooking is finished.

Transfer the meat mixture to an ovenproof casserole dish and on this spread the mashed potatoes.

Mix the Gruyere cheese with the remaining breadcrumbs, sprinkle this mixture over the mashed potatoes and transfer the casserole to an oven preheated to medium until the dish is heated through and the breadcrumb-cheese mixture is golden brown. Serve immediately.

Fanny de Beauharnais, 1738–1813

La Belle Fanny

When Napoleon Bonaparte took Josephine de Beauharnais as his bride, he also took on her entire family. This was no small chore, as the Beauharnais clan boasted quite enough near-lunatics to make life exceedingly difficult. Two of Josephine's uncles were known to have spent huge sums of money in restaurants and bordellos, and one cousin, Jean Paul, specialized in seducing married women and then challenging their cuckolded husbands to duels. He was rumored to have slept with nearly a thousand women and to have sent one hundred and twenty-five of their husbands to their final resting places.

If there was a saving grace to the family, it was Fanny de Beauharnais, Josephine's aunt. A friend noted that "Fanny was equally devoted to good eating and good sex, and was willing to take either wherever she found them." The Goncourt brothers wrote that "although Fanny would welcome any capable male into her bed, even into her eighth decade she maintained a special place in her heart and her bed for sixteen year old boys."

Fanny was a poet, playwright and novelist, with literary pretensions that far outstretched her talents. She suffered a series of catastrophes at the *Comédie Française* and her books were, at best, objects of sometimes polite and sometimes not-so-polite ridicule. One of the few plays that did succeed was *L'Aveugle Par Amour*, valued today primarily because one of the extant copies once stood in Napoleon's personal library and is decorated with a gold imprint of his coat of arms. It is also interesting to note that while Napoleon was in exile he forbade Josephine to visit him but received regular visits from Fanny.

Despite her misfortunes in the literary world, Fanny maintained a solid reputation as a hostess. "Although I am far from averse to the charms of the bedroom, I cannot help but prefer those of the well-set picnic table," she wrote. On one occasion, Fanny arranged a Sunday lawn luncheon for three friends. The repast consisted of two jellied pheasants from Tuscany, a pâté of foie gras made especially for her in Strasbourg, two game pies from Aix-en-Provence, and several bottles of Spanish sparkling wine.

The first of the two dishes that follows was dedicated to Fanny in 1864 by one of the chefs at Paris' famed Bonfinger restaurant. The restaurant, which is still owned by the same family, has changed little since its early days, and this dish is still offered on a regular basis. The second dish, a garnish intended for use with small cuts of meat, was dedicated to Fanny by the great Georges Auguste Escoffier.

Tournedos à la Beauharnaise

FOR THE BEAUHARNAISE SAUCE:
1 Tbsp shallots, chopped
1 sprig of thyme
¼ bay leaf
3 Tbsp tarragon, chopped
2 Tbsp chervil, chopped
¼ cup vinegar
¼ cup white wine
2 eggs, beaten lightly with 1
    Tbsp water
½ cup butter, cut into ½"
    (1 cm) cubes

¼–½ tsp lemon juice
    (optional)
pinch of cayenne pepper
    (optional)
salt and pepper to taste

FOR THE TOURNEDOS:

4 tournedos (medallions of
   fillet of beef)

½ cup butter

24 new potatoes, peeled

1 Tbsp parsley, chopped finely

salt and pepper to taste

Prepare the sauce: In an enameled saucepan combine the shallots, thyme, bay leaf, 2 Tbsp of the tarragon and 1 Tbsp of the chervil. Add a pinch each of salt and pepper, pour over the vinegar and wine and bring to a boil. Continue to boil until reduced by two-thirds. Let cool.

To the saucepan add the eggs and, over a low flame, beat until the eggs begin to thicken. Immediately begin to add all but one small pat of the butter, in small pieces, whisking constantly. Correct the seasoning with salt and pepper and, if desired, lemon juice and cayenne pepper. Strain the sauce and then add the remaining tarragon and chervil. Dab with the remaining butter and keep warm in a double-boiler.

Prepare the main dish: In a flameproof casserole dish heat 5 Tbsp of the butter. To this add the potatoes. Season with salt and sauté until the potatoes are nearly tender. Transfer to an oven that has been preheated to medium-hot and cook until the potatoes are golden in color and are done through, shaking the casserole dish periodically during cooking. Sprinkle over with the parsley.

Season the tournedos with salt and pepper. In a large skillet heat the remaining butter to the point of fragrance and in this rapidly sauté the tournedos so that they will be nicely browned on the outside and remain pink inside. Transfer to a preheated serving platter and garnish with the potatoes. Spoon over some of the Beauharnaise sauce and serve the remaining sauce separately. (Serves 4).

Garniture à la Beauharnaise
Beauharnaise Garnish

This complex garnish consists of very small artichoke hearts filled with Beauharnaise sauce to which tarragon puree has been added. It is served with small potato balls that were browned in butter. The pan juices of the main dish, those diluted with Madeira wine and veal stock and the addition of chopped truffles, serve as the sauce. The garnish is generally used with large cuts of beef.

The Marquis de Sade, 1740–1814

A Man of Marvelous Taste

The name of the Marquis de Sade has long been synonymous with sexual perversion, but starting in 1990, the year that marked the two hundred and fiftieth anniversary of his birth, the reputation of Comte Donatien Alphonse Francois de Sade underwent a remarkable transformation. Today it seems that the French have acquired a new taste for the Divine Marquis and his masterpieces, of which the best known are *Les 120 Journées de Sodome, Justine*, and *La Philosophie dans le Boudoir*.

While awaiting trial in Marseilles in 1772 for "the horrors which he inflicted on a girl," the Marquis outdid himself, giving a ball for some sixty guests and serving them chocolate pastilles infused with the potent aphrodisiac, Spanish fly. Author Louis Petit de Bachaumont wrote that "those who ate the pastilles began to burn with unchaste ardor and to carry on as if in the grip of the most amorous frenzy," and a local newspaper reported that several guests died and others were severely indisposed. Another tale told is that while visiting a bordello in Marseilles, Sade gave the prostitutes an aphrodisiac they mistook for a poison and had his valet sodomize them. One of the women filed a complaint, but because Sade and Letour had already fled to Italy, they were tried in absentia and were hanged "in effigy." This was not the only time Sade

escaped dying. During the revolution Jean-Paul Marat sentenced him to death, but happily for the Marquis, Marat had misspelled his name and a Monsieur de la Salle went to the guillotine in his place.

Even today it is not common knowledge that the Marquis' appetite for fine food was almost as intense as his appetite for rape and sodomy. When he served as a captain in the army during the Seven Years War, his valet and cook, Jacques Letour, was famous among the French generals for his garlic stew, his parsleyed leg of lamb, and his raspberry mousse. Once, in the town of Tours, de Sade's soldiers took possession of a local inn and while other battalions were engaged in battle the Marquis regaled his own troops with a feast of stuffed pheasants, roast beef and smoked hams. His commander, Lieutenant-General Anser, observed in a letter to his wife, "Here is a man with marvelous taste."

Even during his several periods of imprisonment, de Sade managed to dine well. In the Bastille, where he was incarcerated for five years, he whiled away the hours drinking fine Claret and eating truffled oysters. In the asylum at Charenton, where he eventually died, he dined frequently on partridge stuffed with grapes, and in the dungeon at Vincennes he showed a distinct preference for smoked Austrian hams, Parmesan cheese and old Port wines. What he did miss in prison was hot chocolate, and he was known to make many petitions regarding this matter to various prison masters.

Fans of Sade now organize annual festivities in his honor, an opera glorifying his work has been staged in Paris' new opera house at place de la Bastille, and an International Centre for de Sade Studies has opened in Epernay. Perhaps best of all, the chef at Paris' Morot-Gaudry restaurant has devised a new dish that carries his name, *Bœuf à la Marquis de Sade*, which is made by placing "blood-red slices of marinated raw beef on virgin lettuce leaves and spooning a well-whipped mousseline sauce over all." Restaurant critic Jean Gras found the dish "titillating."

Huitres Truffé
Truffled Oysters

48 oysters, removed from their
    shells, with liquids and
    shells discarded
½ lb (225 gr) chicken breast,
    cooked, cooled and cut
    into small cubes
¼ lb (115 gr) bacon, chopped
    coarsely
black pepper to taste
1 oz fresh or tinned truffles cut
    into pea sized rounds

flour as required
4 eggs, lightly beaten with
    2 Tbsp cold water
olive oil for frying
brittany sea salt (kosher salt)
    as required
24 slices white bread, without
    crusts, toasted and cut into
    triangle shaped halves

Using a mortar and pestle or a food processor, grind together the chicken breast, bacon and pepper to form a coarse puree. Add the truffles and mix well by hand.

Cut a slit in each oyster, making a pocket, and fill the pockets with the chicken breast mixture.

Dip each oyster first into flour, then into the beaten eggs and again into the flour, coating well. Transfer the oysters to a large heavy skillet with the oil heated to about 375 degrees Fahrenheit and fry, turning once until the coating has takes on a light golden color. Remove the oysters with a slotted spoon, drain on paper toweling and transfer to a preheated warm oven for 5 minutes. Sprinkle over with salt and serve on toast points. (Serves 6–8 as a first course).

Perdreau Bourguignon
Partridge à la Burgundy

4 partridges, dressed and
    cleaned
3 cups seedless white grapes,
    peeled
2 chorizo sausages, chopped
    finely
3 oz (85 gr) Prosciutto ham,
    chopped finely

5 Tbsp shallots, chopped finely
2 recipes for standard pie crust
4 toasted bread croutons for
    serving
pâté of foie gras for serving
Madeira sauce for serving (see
    below)

TO MAKE THE PARTRIDGES:

In the upper part of a double boiler combine the grapes, sausage, ham and shallots and heat these through over hot water. With this mixture stuff the birds and sew closed. Place the birds in a lightly greased oven pan and bake in a hot oven until tender (30–35 minutes). Remove from the oven and let cool nearly to room temperature.

When the birds are cool cover each individually with pastry crust and return to the oven for 10 minutes longer.

TO PREPARE THE MADEIRA SAUCE:

1 cup any good brown sauce or
    gravy
¼ cup Madeira or dry sherry

1 Tbsp butter
salt and pepper to taste

In a heavy skillet or saucepan combine half of the Madeira with the brown sauce and simmer for 8 to 10 minutes. Stir in the remaining Madeira and bring the sauce just to a boil. Remove from the flame and season lightly with salt and pepper. Add the butter, swirling the saucepan constantly until the butter has melted. Yields about 1 cup.

Spread the croutons with pâté de foie gras and on each crouton set one of the birds. Serve with Madeira sauce in a gravy boat. (Serves 4).

Madame du Barry, 1743–1793
Cherchez la Femme

A prostitute who rose to become the most powerful and wealthy woman in France, the beautiful and vivacious Marie-Jeanne Bécu was born out of wedlock to poor commoners at Vaucouleurs. She came to Paris to seek her fortune and soon found it in the bedrooms of her noble lovers. King Louis XV, lonely and bored after the death of Madame de Pompadour, was enticed by her youth and sexual expertise, and in order to install her in his palace, arranged her marriage to Comte Guillaume du Barry.

Madame du Barry was presented at Versailles in 1769, covered with magnificent diamonds, and her beauty dazzled all. She was also admired by the artists of the era, who painted her portrait and sculpted her in marble, plaster and porcelain. She did not aspire to have power such as Madame de Pompadour had exercised in the affairs of the state; her main occupation was with her toilette. Every morning, as soon as she rose, merchants hastened to bring her silks, laces, embroidery, robes and jewels.

She was also known as a great collector of art, so much so that her rooms at Versailles, as well as her pavilion in Louveciennes, soon become museums, boasting marvelous Sèvres vases with goats' heads, teapots with green ribbons and golden hatchings, basins with trellises and birds and much more. It is estimated that between 1769 and 1774 the king spent almost four million *livres*, about twenty-four million dollars in today's terms, on his mistress.

Upon the sudden death of the king in 1774, Louis XVI ascended the throne and his wife, Marie Antoinette, who regarded Madame du Barry as "the silliest and most impertinent creature alive," banished her from the palace. At the age of fifty, du Barry was condemned to death by the Revolutionary Tribunal and sent to the guillotine. Her famous last words were addressed to the executioner, "Monsieur, one little instant more!"

The countess was an able cook, and designed many suppers for the king. Once, when Louis XV declared in her presence that only men make great chefs, she invited him to an intimate supper prepared by her *cuisiniere*. It was a great success and the king exclaimed, "Who is the new man you have cooking for you? He is as good as any cook in the royal household." "It's a woman cook, Your Majesty," Madame du Barry replied, "and I think you should honour her with nothing less than the *Cordon-bleu*." This title, which originated in the sixteenth-century *Ordre du Saint Esprit*, whose members were called *Cordon-bleus* after the broad blue ribbons they wore, was applied in the eighteenth century to anyone who excelled, and in particular to fine cooks.

Several chefs, including the great La Chapelle, named dishes after du Barry, and nearly all those dishes contain cauliflower.

Crème du Barry
Cream of Cauliflower Soup du Barry

1½ lb (675 gr) cauliflower, divided into florets	5 cups chicken stock
6 Tbsp each butter and flour	2 egg yolks
1¼ cups milk	¼ cup whipping cream
	salt and white pepper to taste

Bring a large pot of lightly salted water to a boil. Measure 1 cup of the cauliflower florets into a small bowl and reserve. Place the remaining florets in the boiling water, return to the boil and then reduce the flame and let simmer for 10 minutes. Drain and set the cauliflower aside.

Distribute the reserved florets on a baking sheet and place them in an oven that has been preheated to medium, until they become lightly golden (20–25 minutes).

In a large saucepan melt the butter. Remove from the flame and blend in the flour. Add the milk and chicken stock, mixing well, return to the flame and cook, stirring regularly, until the mixture has thickened somewhat (about 5 minutes).

Transfer the boiled cauliflower into a food processor and puree. Add this puree to the saucepan and heat for 1–2 minutes. In a small bowl whisk the yolks and sweet cream together and then add these to the soup. Season with salt and white pepper to taste. Transfer the soup to a large soup tureen or into individual soup plates, garnishing with the roasted cauliflower. Serve at once. (Serves 4–6).

Artichauts du Barry
Artichokes du Barry

FOR THE ARTICHOKES:
10–12 artichoke hearts, cooked
1 small cauliflower, divided
    into florets

salt and white pepper to taste
1 oz (30 gr) butter

FOR THE SAUCE:
2 Tbsp butter
2 Tbsp flour
⅔ cup milk

¼ lb (115 gr) Gruyere or
    Emmenthal cheese, grated
salt and pepper
    to taste

Immerse the cauliflower florets in rapidly boiling salted water. Reduce the heat to a medium simmer and cook until the florets are just tender (about 10 minutes).

In a large saucepan melt the butter and over a low flame heat the artichoke hearts through in the butter.

Prepare the sauce: In a fresh saucepan melt the butter and into this stir the flour, cooking for 1–2 minutes, stirring constantly. Remove from the flame and gradually add the milk, again stirring constantly. Return to the heat, bring to the boil still stirring, and cook for 3–4 minutes. Remove from the heat, stir in half the cheese and season to taste with salt and pepper.

Place the artichokes in a buttered ovenproof casserole dish, top each with a cauliflower floret and spoon the sauce over. Sprinkle with the remaining cheese and place in an oven that has been preheated to medium until the cheese has melted and lightly browned (10–15 minutes). (Serves 4–6 as a first course).

Sorbet du Barry

3.3 lbs (1½ kilos) bananas, cut into chunks

2 small pineapples, cut into chunks, or 2 tins of pineapple chunks, drained

2 oranges, peeled and cut into sections

2 lemons, peeled and cut into sections

2 Tbsp lemon juice

1 cup confectioners' sugar

1 egg white

Puree the fruits with the juice and sugar in a blender or food processor, adding more sugar to taste if necessary. Transfer the puree to a large flat metal dish and freeze until nearly solid. Remove from the freezer and beat the mixture until fluffy. Add the egg white and beat for 1 minute longer. Return to the freezer. Once again, before the mixture is solid remove from the freezer and beat well. Transfer to an ice cream mold or individual dessert glasses, return to the freezer and freeze solid. Transfer the sorbet to the regular refrigeration compartment about 15 minutes before serving. (Serves 6–8).

The Count of Mirabeau, 1749–1791

Revolutionary Dreams

To Robespierre, the ideal outcome of the French revolution would have been a universal diet of lentils. Danton, more of a gourmet, felt that in the "universal freedom to come" Frenchmen should dine on pheasant stuffed with truffles in cream sauce. The Count de Mirabeau, perhaps a bit more realistic, thought that all French men and women should dine generously at least four times a day.

Honoré Gabriel Riqueti, Count de Mirabeau was an unlikely candidate to have become the most prominent voice of the revolution in its first years. Born into a noble Provençal family, by the time he was twenty he had abandoned his cavalry regiment, piled up an unbelievable collection of debts, and implicated himself in numerous adultery scandals. He was repeatedly imprisoned and spent several years in the cells of Chateau d'If and in the dungeons of Vincennes. On one occasion he was even sentenced to death but managed to get the sentence reversed.

While imprisoned he wrote essays and novels, including the sensational *Essai sur le Despotisme*, various erotic novels and several minor historical novels. In 1780, following his release, he was elected a delegate to the National Assembly on behalf of the commoners, and soon became

a central figure in the revolutionary scene. "We will not yield but to bayonets," his answer to the king's ultimatum about the arrangements of the new Assembly, is remembered as a pivotal moment in French history. Above all, he was an extraordinary orator; his speeches bewitched his fellow delegates as well as the people in the streets of Paris.

In prison or in power, in exile or in glory, Mirabeau, a gourmet with exquisite taste, always made sure to dine well. In his cell at the Chateau d'If he received regular supplies of geese stuffed with truffles, fresh strawberries and fine Port wine. At Vincennes he dined regularly on trout, fine cheeses from Italy, and cakes baked for him by one of his lovers in Paris. At the height of his popularity, he was frequently found at the Tour d'Argent, where he dined on duck in orange sauce; at Le Doyen, where he would meet his lady friends and feast on oysters; or at Procope where he would review his speeches (nearly all of which were ghost-written for him by Etienne Dumont) while sipping coffee and eating orange sorbet.

Mirabeau's favorite restaurants are still open. The following dish was dedicated to him by one of the chefs at Procope, probably in 1790, a year before his death, and is still popular today in this charming establishment, the oldest café in Paris.

Entrecôte Mirabeau

4 entrecote steaks, trimmed and lightly flattened	24 large green or black olives, pitted
½ cup butter, at room temperature	½ cup tarragon leaves
18 anchovy fillets	3 Tbsp olive oil
	salt and pepper to taste

Several hours before cooking the steaks, prepare the butter by crushing 6 of the anchovy fillets with a fork and then blending them together with the butter. Form the butter into eight squares and refrigerate.

In two separate saucepans bring lightly salted water to a rapid boil. Reduce the flame and in one of the saucepans simmer the olives gently for 4–5 minutes. Plunge the tarragon leaves into the other saucepan and simmer for 3–4 minutes. Drain both.

Brush the steaks with the oil and season to taste with salt and pepper. Cook the steaks under a hot grill for 1 minute. Turn the steaks and cook 1 minute longer. Turn again and cook until the steaks are done to taste. To serve, arrange the steaks on preheated plates and garnish with the remaining anchovies, olives and tarragon leaves. On each steak place two balls of the anchovy butter and serve immediately. (Serves 4).

Antoine Beauvilliers, 1754–1817

A Table for Two

P residing over his restaurant in courtly dress that invariably included a sword and frilled shirt, Antoine Beauvilliers, who spoke five languages, was minutely aware of every political and social nuance of the day, and knew precisely where to seat ambassadors and ministers, royalists and republicans, all of whom he would welcome by name.

Beauvilliers, who prior to the opening of his restaurant in 1782 served as chef to the Count of Provence, the future King Louis XVIII, was the first to introduce the novelty of listing all available dishes on a menu, and serving them at small, individual tables during fixed hours. Previously, innkeepers offered their clients food from the owner's table, and it was only in 1765 that the first public dining room was opened in Paris, by a soup vendor named Boulanger. This establishment was soon followed by other simple soup and ragout restaurants, whose few offerings were written on a board and served on long tables shared by strangers.

rue Monsieur-le-Prince, and the third is for a garnish that was part of the menu at La Grande Taverne, and today is served primarily at restaurants adhering to the rules of haute cuisine.

Gâteau Beauvilliers
Beauvilliers Cake

4 cups sugar
1½ cups chopped almonds
5 egg whites, unbeaten
4 eggs
1¾ cups each plain flour, rice flour and potato flour
7 egg whites, beaten stiff

3 Tbsp kirsch liqueur
1 Tbsp lemon juice
confectioners' sugar as required
2 cups highest-quality vanilla ice cream

In a heavy saucepan make a sugar syrup by dissolving 1 cup of the sugar in 2 cups of hot water. Bring to a boil, stirring regularly, let boil for 2–3 minutes and then remove from the flame. Set aside for later use.

With a mortar and pestle or with a food processor, pound together the almonds and 1½ cups of the sugar until the mixture is extremely fine. Then add the unbeaten egg whites a little at a time. Rub this mixture through a sieve.

In a mixing bowl blend together the remaining sugar and the whole eggs. When completely smooth add the almond mixture and each of the flours. Fold in the stiff egg whites and transfer the mixture to a 10 cup ring mold which has been lightly sprinkled with potato flour. Bake in an oven that has been preheated to low until the cake is done (about 30 minutes). To test to see if the cake is done, insert a toothpick. If the toothpick comes out clean, the cake is done. Let the cake cool.

While the cake is cooling prepare the icing by heating the syrup you made earlier to about 250 degrees Fahrenheit (130 degrees Celsius). Transfer the syrup to a pre-warmed bowl and then add the kirsch, lemon juice and enough of the confectioners' sugar to produce a fairly stiff paste. With this mixture immediately ice the cake and then fill the center with the ice cream. (Serves 8).

Garniture à la Beauvilliers
Beauvilliers Garnish

A classic compound garnish devised by Beauvilliers to accompany small cuts of beef or lamb.

FOR THE KROMESKIES:

6 crêpes (follow the instructions for making crêpes on p. 303)

1½ cups boiled spinach, drained well and chopped finely

3–4 Tbsp butter, melted

breadcrumbs as required

oil for deep frying

FOR THE BRAISED CELERY:

6 stalks celery, without leaves, scraped and well washed

2 cups chicken stock

salt and pepper to taste

3 Tbsp butter

FOR THE STUFFED TOMATOES:

1 calf's brain, cleaned thoroughly and quartered

3 cups chicken stock

5 Tbsp butter or Béchamel sauce (see p. 67)

8 small tomatoes, halved and with the pulp scooped out and discarded

3 Tbsp dried breadcrumbs

To prepare the kromeskies: divide the spinach on the crêpes, spreading evenly and then roll the crêpes, and slice them crosswise into 1″ lengths. Dip the crêpes sections first into the butter and then into the breadcrumbs, coating well. Fry in deep oil heated to 375 degrees Fahrenheit (190 degrees Celsius) just until the breadcrumbs brown, and remove with a slotted spoon to drain on paper towels.

To prepare the celery: cut the stalks in half lengthwise, and then into 1″ (2½ cm) lengths. In a saucepan heat the chicken stock and in this boil the celery for 3–4 minutes. Remove the celery with a slotted spoon, season to taste with salt and pepper and in a saucepan sauté in the butter for an additional 2–3 minutes.

To prepare the brain: bring the chicken stock to a boil and into this plunge the brain, cooking for 3–4 minutes. Drain and rub through a fine sieve. In the top section of a *bain-marie* heat this puree over boiling water while stirring in the 3 Tbsp of the butter or Béchamel sauce. With this mixture fill the hollowed out tomatoes. Sprinkle over the breadcrumbs and then the remaining butter and finish under a hot grill just until the breadcrumbs begin to brown. (Serves 4–6).

Soufflé à la Beauvilliers

Before preparing this dish, read the hints on making soufflé that follow the recipe.

⅔ cup sugar
8 egg yolks, lightly beaten
½ cup Benedictine or Grand
    Marnier liqueur

10 egg whites
¼ tsp cream of tartar
butter and sugar (to prepare
    the soufflé dish)

In a double boiler, over but not in hot water, beat together the sugar and egg yolks until the mixture is smooth and forms a broad ribbon as it runs from a lifted spoon. Add the liqueur and immediately transfer the mixture to a bowl over ice and there continue to beat until the mixture is cooled.

In a separate bowl combine the egg whites and cream of tartar and beat until stiff but not dry. Fold the egg yolk mixture into the beaten whites and then transfer the mixture to an 8″ (20 cm) soufflé dish that has been well greased and then dusted lightly with sugar. Bake as instructed (see hints, on following page) until done (12–15 minutes). Serve at once. (Serves 6–8).

Hints for Preparing a Soufflé

—Egg whites should be beaten by hand with a whisk or with an electric beater. Do not beat them in a food processor. Be sure that the bowl in which you beat the eggs is neither greasy nor damp. If the whites do not stiffen, add ¼ tsp of cream of tartar and continue beating.

—Once beaten, the egg whites should be stiff enough to form upright peaks when lifted on the wire of the beater.

—To bake soufflés, preheat the oven to hot. Place the soufflé on a rack in the center of the oven and, as soon as you put the soufflé in the oven reduce the temperature to medium-hot.

—When a soufflé is done, it will raise 2–3″ (5–8 cm) over the rim of the mold and will be browned on top. To test for doneness, plunge a thin knife into the center through the side of the puff. When the knife comes out clean, the soufflé is done.

—A well cooked soufflé will stay puffy for about 5 minutes if left in the turned-off oven. As it cools it will begin to sink, so serve the soufflé as soon as possible.

Talleyrand, 1754–1838

On the Table

Charles Maurice de Talleyrand-Périgord, one of France's truly great gourmets, considered the luxury of his table to be a vital element in his unique career as the most prominent European diplomat of his time, although others might argue that it was actually the absolute absence of any moral scruples that allowed him to survive the French Revolution, the Directory, the Empire and the Restoration.

Talleyrand had two guiding principles. The first he expressed in a letter to a friend: "Never let religion or morality interfere with your career or personal pleasure." He shared the second with his chef: "The secret of survival is obvious—give good dinners and stay in the good graces of women."

Even though he was appointed Abbot of Saint-Remi de Reims at the age of twenty-five, and became Bishop of Autun at thirty-four, church business never stopped Talleyrand from leading a dissipated worldly life. It was during Napoleon's reign, when he served as foreign minister and entertained the crème de la crème of European society that Talleyrand's exquisite sense of taste found an equal match in the great chef Antonin Carême. Together they presented the finest table in all of Europe. Some have gone so far as to speculate that the magnificent

dinners given by Talleyrand at the Congress of Vienna in 1814 were instrumental in gaining favorable terms for France.

Talleyrand was convinced that the best way to conduct state business was at the dinner table. To make certain that his table was faultless he conferred with Carême every morning, planning the evening's dinner. In his diary Carême wrote that his employer insisted on using only the finest and freshest products, and that dinners of forty-eight courses were not uncommon. "I have designed them and I have seen them served. Who has not seen such a dinner has seen nothing at all," he wrote.

Always an optimist, when he was excommunicated from the Catholic Church for supporting the confiscation of church property by the government, Talleyrand wrote to the Duc de Lauzun: "You have heard the news: excommunicated. Come and dine to console me. Everyone refuses me fire and water; so we will eat nothing but glazed cold meats and drink only chilled wines and we shall drink coffee black as the devil, hot as hell, pure as an angel and sweet as love"

The following dish was dedicated to Talleyrand by Jules Montagne, the chef in charge of preparing hors d'œuvres under Carême. The second dish is generally attributed to Carême himself.

Paupiettes d'Anchois à la Talleyrand
Rolled Anchovies à la Talleyrand

12 fresh anchovy fillets	2 Tbsp truffles, finely chopped
1 romaine lettuce, with the coarse leaves discarded	4 hard boiled eggs cut in thick slices
butter as required	3 Tbsp mayonnaise
salt and pepper to taste	1 Tbsp olive oil
½ cup of pickled tuna fish, well chilled	lemon wedges and slices of beets for garnish

Shred the lettuce leaves and then weigh them. For every ½ lb of lettuce melt 3 Tbsp of butter in a skillet. Season the lettuce with salt and pepper and add to the skillet. Cook gently just until the liquids are evaporated. Set aside to keep warm.

Rub the tuna and truffles through a fine sieve and mix them

together until the mixture is smooth. Add the mayonnaise and mix well. Spoon this mixture onto the fish fillets and then roll the fillets, fastening if necessary with a toothpick.

Place each fillet on a slice of the hard boiled egg and transfer to a small serving plate. Surround with the *chiffonade* of lettuce, sprinkle over the olive oil and decorate the plates with lemon wedges and beet slices. (Serves 6 as a first course).

Petites Croustades à la Talleyrand
Pastry Shells à la Talleyrand

FOR THE CROUSTADES:

6 round bread rolls

3 eggs lightly whisked with 2 tsp water

oil for deep frying

FOR THE SWEETBREADS:

2 Tbsp each onions, carrots, celery and ham, all finely diced

2 Tbsp butter

1 small bouquet garni made by tying together 2 sprigs parsley, 2 sprigs thyme and ½ bay leaf

salt to taste

pinch of pepper

1 lb (450 gr) sweetbreads, soaked, peeled and trimmed

2 Tbsp dry white wine

½ cup beef or chicken stock or consommé

FOR THE PERIGUEUX SAUCE:

1 cup *demi-glace* or Espagnole sauce (see p. 94)

½ cup Madeira wine

1 Tbsp butter

salt and pepper to taste

2 Tbsp truffles, chopped

Prepare the croustades: Cut the tops off the bread rolls and hollow them out, leaving a firm shell intact. Coat the rolls, inside and out with the egg. Also brush the tops of the rolls with eggs and then deep fry the rolls and the tops in hot oil until golden brown. Set aside to keep warm.

Prepare the sauce: In a heavy skillet or saucepan combine half of the Madeira with the Espagnole sauce and simmer for 8–10 minutes. Stir in the remaining Madeira and bring the sauce just to a boil. Remove from the flame and season lightly with salt and pepper. Stir in the truffles, add the butter and swirl the saucepan constantly until the butter has melted. Set aside to keep warm.

Prepare the sweetbreads: In a skillet melt the butter and in this cook the diced vegetables and ham over a low heat with the herb bouquet and a generous pinch of salt and pepper until the vegetables are tender but not browned (10–15 minutes).

Season the sweetbreads with salt, arrange them in the skillet and baste them with the butter and vegetables. Cover and cook over a low flame for 5 minutes. Turn, baste again and cook 5 minutes longer, adding butter if the skillet dries out. Transfer the sweetbreads to a small flameproof casserole dish. Pour the wine into the skillet and boil down over a high flame until the liquids are reduced to ½ cup. Pour these liquids over the sweetbreads, vegetables and bouquet garni, and then add just enough bouillon to barely cover. Bring to a simmer, cover the casserole dish and transfer to an oven preheated to low. Adjust the oven temperature so that the liquids barely simmer for 45 minutes.

To prepare the dish, discard the bouquet garni, divide the sweetbreads in the croustades, spoon over some of the Perigueux sauce, cover with the tops of the croustades, spoon over a bit more of the sauce and serve with the remaining sauce in a sauceboat. (Serves 6 as a first course).

Jean Anthelme Brillat-Savarin, 1755–1826

You Are What You Eat

In the pantheon of France's great gastronomes, no name shines more brightly than that of Jean Anthelme Brillat-Savarin. Born at Belley as Jean Anthelme Brillat, he added the second surname on the death of an aunt who left him her entire fortune. A man of many talents, Brillat-Savarin was a lawyer, a physician and a magistrate as well as a politician. During the Reign of Terror he fled to Switzerland, traveled through England and eventually spent three years in the United States.

He considered the Swiss "eminently civilized, but fools because they have no time for pleasure," thought the English "snobs with no appreciation for the finer things of life" and he found the Americans to be "charming barbarians." While in the United States he divided his time between Connecticut, where he was invited often to turkey shoots and to feast on oyster-stuffed turkeys, and New York, where for a while he was first violin in an orchestra at the Park Theater.

After his return to Paris he devoted himself to the compilation of *La Physiologie du Goût* (*The Physiology of Taste*), an eight volume encyclopedic work that upon publication was immediately acknowledged as a masterpiece. The book, originally published at his own expense in 1825, when he was seventy years old, was the first work to treat dining as a form of art, and gastronomy as a form of science, "the intelligent knowledge of whatever concerns man's nourishment." Many modern chefs believe that it was with this work that Brillat-Savarin forever separated gourmets from gluttons.

Dedicated to the concept that everything, from personal well-being to the fate of nations, depended on nourishment, Brillat-Savarin, who had the habit of eating two dozens oyster for breakfast, included hundreds of aphorisms in his book. The most famous include: "tell me what you eat and I shall tell you what you are"; "a dessert course without cheese is like a beautiful woman with only one eye"; and "the truffle is not a positive aphrodisiac but it can, in certain situations, make women more tender and men more agreeable."

Brillat-Savarin invented more than three hundred dishes. "The discovery of a new dish," he said, "does more for human happiness than the discovery of a star." He named numerous dishes after his mother Aurore, and many more carry his own name. He may also be the only gastronome with the privilege of having a cheese named after him, the Brillat-Savarin cheese, which was created in the 1930s by Henri Androuet. This is a soft, white, cows' milk cheese that has a thick and velvety white crust and boasts a remarkable 75% fat content.

The first dish that follows was created by Brillat-Savarin himself, and the second was dedicated to him in 1825 by the great chef Carême. The cake that carries his name originated in Alsace and was named after him by a chef in the village of Rouffach.

Omelette Savarin

12 eggs
2–3 Tbsp carp roe
3 oz (85 gr) fresh tuna, minced
1 shallot, minced
4 Tbsp butter + 4 Tbsp butter, softened

1 Tbsp chives, cut finely
1 Tbsp parsley, chopped finely
2 Tbsp milk
2 oz (60 gr) clarified butter
1 lemon

With a whisk, mix together the softened butter, chives and parsley. Rinse and trim the roe and then blanch in salted water for 5 minutes. Drain and chop. In a saucepan, over a medium heat, mix together the roe, tuna, shallot and the butter, taking care that the roe and tuna do not brown.

In a mixing bowl beat the eggs lightly with the milk. Add the roe mixture and mix together well. In a large heavy skillet heat the clarified butter and in this cook the omelet until done.

Place the herbed butter into a pre-heated serving dish, ideally one with a depression in the middle and over this squeeze the lemon. When the omelet is ready turn it out onto the herb butter. Serve immediately. (Serves 6).

Consommé Brillat-Savarin

½ large chicken breast, skinned and boned

salt, pepper and marjoram to taste

6 Tbsp butter

1¼ cups flour, sifted

2 eggs

1 cup milk, boiled down by ⅓

leaves of ½ very young bib or leaf lettuce

½ romaine lettuce

¼ cup sorrel leaves, chopped

2 Tbsp chervil leaves, chopped

8 cups chicken consommé

3½ tsp tapioca

¼ cup dry Sherry wine

Season the chicken breast with salt, pepper and marjoram. In a skillet melt 2 Tbsp of the butter and in this sauté the breast over a medium heat until cooked through (allow 6–8 minutes for each side). Remove from the skillet, let cool several minutes and cut into thin julienne slices.

Make a batter by combining the flour and eggs. Season with ¾ tsp of salt and then add the boiled milk. Mix until an even fluid batter is attained. Butter a heavy skillet or crêpe pan and pour in a very thin layer of batter. Cook until this very thin pancake is browned on one side, and then turn to the other side and cook until browned. Make three crêpes in all. Let these cool for several minutes and cut into rounds about 2 cm in diameter.

Slice the lettuce leaves finely. In a skillet melt ¼ cup more of the butter and to this add the lettuce, sorrel and chervil leaves. Season with salt and pepper and cook gently until the liquids are evaporated.

In a saucepan bring the consommé to a boil, and then sprinkle in the tapioca. Boil gently for 18 minutes, stirring regularly, and then strain through a muslin cloth or fine sieve. Transfer to a clean saucepan, stir in the sherry and bring just to the point of boiling. To serve, garnish the soup with the crêpe circles, julienned chicken and *chiffonade* of lettuce. (Serves 6).

Savarin

FOR THE CAKE:

¼ oz. dry yeast

¼ cup lukewarm milk

9 oz (250 gr) flour, sifted

3 eggs

pinch each of salt and sugar

3 oz (85 gr) butter, softened

1 cup apricot jam

FOR THE SYRUP:

1 quart (1 liter) water

½ lb (225 gr) sugar

rind of 1 lemon and 1 orange

1 stick cinnamon about 2″
    (5 cm) long

¼ cup rum or Grand Marnier
    liqueur

Whipped cream for serving

Fresh fruit salad for serving

In a large bowl combine the yeast and milk. Add the flour, salt and sugar and mix together well. Then add the eggs one at a time, working constantly with a spatula until the dough is thick and elastic. Add the butter, mix thoroughly, cover the mixture with a towel and set aside in a warm spot to rise for 10 minutes. Punch the dough down, then let it recover and stand another 10 minutes.

Pour the dough into a buttered flute mold, filling the mold to ⅔ of its capacity and let stand to rise for 30–40 minutes. Transfer to an oven that has been preheated to medium hot, until done (20–25 minutes). Unmold onto a wire rack and let cool.

Prepare the syrup by combining the water and sugar and bringing to a boil. Let boil for 5–7 minutes, remove from the flame and then add the rum or Grand Marnier, cinnamon and orange and lemon rind, mixing well.

With a skewer about ¼″ (½ cm) in diameter punch holes throughout the top of the cake and drip the syrup into the holes until the cake is saturated. Coat the top of the cake generously with apricot jam and serve garnished with whipped cream and fresh fruit salad. (Serves 6).

Grimod de la Reynière, 1758–1837

Food for Thought

A lawyer by profession, Alexandre Balthazar Laurent Grimod de la Reynière established a multi-faceted reputation as a gourmet with exquisite taste, a writer with an irreverent but charming sense of humor, and a sometimes scoundrel. Born in Paris into a noble family, his hands were congenitally deformed and all his life he had to wear gloved prostheses. Reynière was fond of the theater and of theatrical gestures. He was known, for example, to host lunches to which the guests were admitted only after they had consumed seventeen cups of coffee, and, on one occasion, he emulated his own funeral repast with a lavish dinner.

With the emergence of modern restaurants in the post revolutionary period, Reynière became the first person to fill the role of restaurant critic and thus he is remembered today as the father of modern food journalism. Between 1803 and 1812, he published a periodical, *l'Almanach des Gourmands*, in which he evaluated cafés and restaurants, offering opinions and detailing prices and addresses. He gathered a jury of tasters that awarded certificates to various chefs and restaurants, and also published their judgments in the almanac. Its annual editions constituted a valuable part of every gastronome's library until the famous gourmet was accused of "interested partiality." It turned out that Grimod was not above accepting the occasional bribe. Although this forced him to cease publication of the periodical he lost none of his popularity.

Reynière was a master of aphorisms. His most famous aphorism appeared in his manual for hosts, *Le Manuel des Amphitryons*, published in 1808, where he writes that "a host who can neither carve nor serve is like the owner of a fine library who cannot read." Another memorable aphorism of his warns that the "aphrodisiac property of celery" makes it "not in any way a food for bachelors." Nevertheless, the man who claimed that "a fine sauce will make even an elephant or a grandfather palatable" never had a shortage of invitations to the best homes and restaurants of the city.

Cotes de Veau Hachées Grimod de la Reynière Minced Veal Chops Grimod de la Reynière

8 thick veal chops
¾ lb (350 gr) green asparagus
    tips
½ tsp salt
breadcrumbs as required
1 cup milk
2 Tbsp mushrooms, chopped
    finely

nutmeg to taste
3 eggs beaten lightly with 2 tsp
    water
¾ cup butter, melted
2 cups beef or veal stock
salt and pepper to taste

Place the asparagus tips in a saucepan and pour over cold water just to cover. Add ½ tsp salt, cover and bring to the boil. Immediately reduce the flame and simmer until the asparagus tips are barely tender (6–8 minutes). Remove from the flame and let the tips stand in the liquid.

Cut the meat off the bones of the chops and chop the meat finely, reserving the bones. Weigh the meat. Weigh out ¼ of the weight of the meat in breadcrumbs and soak these in the milk for 2–3 minutes and then squeeze dry by hand. In a mixing bowl combine the chopped meat, breadcrumbs and mushrooms. Mix well and season to taste with salt, pepper and nutmeg.

Place the bones on waxed paper, and with the meat and bread-crumb mixture reshape the chops on the bones. Coat with the beaten egg mixture and then with dry breadcrumbs. In a heavy skillet melt ¼ cup of the butter and in this fry the reconstructed chops, handling carefully at all times with two spatulas to preserve the shape.

While the chops are cooking, move the stock into a saucepan and boil until reduced to ⅓ of its original volume. To serve, place the chops on individual serving plates and surround these with the concentrated stock. Drain the asparagus, dip them in ¼ cup of the remaining melted butter and place these around the chops. In a small saucepan, over a high flame, boil the remaining butter just until it turns brown. Pour the browned butter over the chops and serve immediately. (Serves 4).

Poulet Grimod de la Reynière
Chicken Grimod de la Reynière

1 chicken, about 3½ lb (1½ kilos), trussed
9 cups chicken stock
½ small cabbage, shredded
2 carrots, chopped
1 medium onion, chopped

2 cups sweet cream
2¼ lb (1 kilo) shrimps, in their shells
¼ cup butter
¾ cup Parmesan cheese, grated
salt and pepper to taste

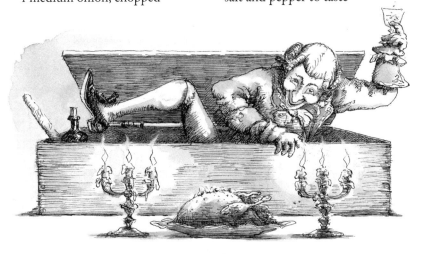

Place the chicken in a large saucepan with 6 cups of the stock, the cabbage, carrots and onion. Poach the chicken by bringing the liquids to a boil, skimming the surface well and then simmering gently until the bird is done. To test for doneness, prick a thigh. When the juice that runs out is white, the bird will be done. Remove the chicken from the liquids, discard the string and set the bird aside to keep warm.

In a saucepan boil the remaining stock over a medium-high flame until it is reduced to ½ its original volume. Continue to cook, adding the sweet cream slowly and stirring constantly with a wooden spoon, until the mixture is quite thick. Remove this sauce from the flame and season to taste with salt and pepper.

Drop the shrimp into a saucepan of rapidly boiling water. Lower the flame and simmer just until the shrimp turn pink (about 3–4 minutes), taking care not to overcook. Drain immediately and run briefly under cold water. Peel the shrimps and chop them finely. Reserve and set aside ½ cup of the chopped shrimps.

Blend into the larger portion of shrimps 2 cups of the sauce and with this mixture fill the cavity of the chicken, packing the mixture in tightly.

Using a mortar and pestle or food processor, process the reserved shrimp into a fine paste and then blend this together with the butter. Add the pounded shrimp to the remaining sauce and heat the sauce through. Strain the sauce and keep warm until ready for use.

Sprinkle the bird with a few teaspoons of the sauce, sprinkle over the cheese and place under a hot grill just until the top is nicely browned. Serve at once, with the sauce served in a gravy boat. (Serves 4–6).

King George IV, 1762–1830

Extreme Appetites

In 1810, the archbishop of Canterbury described the Prince of Wales and future King George IV, George Augustus Frederick, as "a man who eats, drinks and fornicates so indiscriminately that he makes all Englishmen look foolish." Being a charitable and hopeful man, he added that "we do hope however that in time he will modify his behavior."

The archbishop's charity was, however, wasted. A year later, the prince's first notable act as regent to his insane father, King George III, was to invite two thousand guests for a sumptuous banquet. Emulating the excesses of Louis XIV of France in Versailles, he had an artificial stream created for the festivities, the water springing from a silver fountain in front of his own chair. The stream ran through a channel in the garden and was spanned by thirty-five small bridges, each made of solid silver. One guest wrote in her diary that "even though everyone ate well, no one ate nearly as much as his Highness, who consumed thirty-six oysters, a kilo each of Russian sturgeon and Iranian caviar, eleven quails and three partridges."

Even though times were difficult and many of his subjects were hungry, the prince spent a fortune on his mistresses, on lavish

entertaining and grandiose architectural projects. His greatest extravaganza was the Brighton Pavilion, an Oriental pleasure palace that became the center of his unorthodox activities. On one occasion the prince invited two male friends to a dinner he hosted for sixteen Parisian prostitutes, serving them venison from Canada, fish from the Caribbean, partridges from India and asparagus from the Loire Valley. The huge kitchens in the palace, equipped to serve as many as fifteen hundred people at once, had the most modern cooking equipment of the time, making it possible to roast eight tons of meat and bake as many as four thousand cakes in a single day.

In 1816, the prince hired the services of French chef Carême, considered by many to be the greatest chef in history, but lost him after a mere nine months. Carême told his employer that the damp climate of England was destroying his health, but in his memoirs he wrote that the prince was "constantly after me to name one of my dishes after him, but in good conscience I could not dedicate anything to a man who did little more than make a pig of himself at the dining table." His successor, a Spanish chef from Mallorca, whose name has been lost to history, had no such reservations, dedicating to the prince the following dish, a marvelous first course ideally accompanied by a sweet Sauterne wine.

George Peaches

1 lb (450 gr) ripe peaches
small leaves of red or green
   lettuce, as required

1 cup mayonnaise
½ cup sweet cream
1 cup chopped almonds

Drop the peaches into a pot of rapidly boiling water for 30 seconds. Remove the peaches with a slotted spoon and then peel the skins. Cut each peach in half, remove the pits and then cut each half into 4 slices lengthways.

Place the peach slices in a saucepan and pour over lightly salted boiling water until they are just covered. Simmer gently until the peaches are tender (about 5 minutes). Drain the peaches and let them cool.

Arrange the lettuce leaves around the edge of a serving dish and pile the peach slices in the center of the dish. Beat together the mayonnaise and sweet cream and pour this sauce over the peaches. Sprinkle with the almonds and serve immediately. (Serves 6–8 as a first course).

Prince Pyotr Bagration, 1765–1812

Battle Rations

W hen Karl von Clausewitz, the great military strategist of the nineteenth century, wrote that "there are generals who win battles and there are those who dine well. The two activities rarely go hand-in-hand," he was probably thinking of Prince Pyotr Ivanovich Bagration.

A descendant of an ancient Georgian royal dynasty, Bagration served in the Russian army as a general under Tsar Alexander I, winning accolades from his commanding officers for his impressive tactical skills and bravery in military campaigns in the Caucasus, against the Turks, and particularly in the Napoleonic wars, from Marengo to Austerlitz to Borodino. Even though he succeeded in repelling the French troops and causing them heavy losses on several occasions, Napoleon once remarked that he always looked forward to his battles with Bagration because "the man is an absolute fool who has not the slightest idea of how to command an army."

Despite his military losses, Bagration declared all of his battles victorious, and celebrated those victories of the mind with extravagant dinners, some of which are immortalized in Tolstoy's *War and Peace*. In 1812, after a battle that cost him more than six hundred of his soldiers, he celebrated his "victory" by hosting three separate parties—one for

his soldiers, one for the villagers, and one for a group of fifty friends he had invited from Saint Petersburg. Historian Nikolas Prut wrote that "the food was marvelous, the drink was plentiful and the Prince made appearances at each of his parties, eating and drinking heartily throughout the festivities. The villagers, so impressed with his flamboyance and kindness, voted to make him an honorary citizen for life."

The prince also enjoyed dining in his palace in Saint Petersburg, where, for a time, the great chef Carême was in charge of his kitchens. The prince and princess hosted fabulous dinners, often inviting three or four hundred guests to eight course meals. Carême, who stayed in Russia for three years, was concerned with the Napoleonic wars only inasmuch as they interfered with his ability to purchase Normandy butter, Loire Valley asparagus, and Bresse chickens. Bagration himself did not live to enjoy a quiet retirement, dying of his wounds at the battle of Borodino.

Potage Bagration

1 cup clarified butter	3 egg yolks
6 Tbsp flour	salt and pepper
1 lb (450 gr) lean veal cut into small dice	1½ cups cooked macaroni, chopped
4 cups chicken consommé	Parmesan cheese, grated, for serving
½ cup sweet cream	

In a small skillet over a very low flame melt ½ cup of the butter. Remove from the flame, let the butter stand for 2–3 minutes and then skim off the white solids from the surface. Gently pour the remaining liquids into a clean saucepan. Over a very low flame add the flour to the butter and stir constantly with a wooden spoon for 5 minutes. Remove from the flame and let stand until ready for use.

In a skillet heat 2 Tbsp of the remaining butter and in this sauté the veal until lightly browned.

In a saucepan combine the butter and flour mixture with the consommé and veal. Simmer gently until the veal is well cooked.

With a slotted spoon remove the veal and pound it finely in a mortar. Return the veal to the soup and then rub the entire mixture through a sieve. Heat just to boiling and then remove immediately from the flame.

Mix together the egg yolks and cream and add this to the soup. Stir constantly over a low flame, until the soup thickens slightly; take care not to boil again. Correct the seasoning with salt and pepper to taste, add the remaining butter and stir until the mixture is uniform throughout. Spoon over the macaroni and serve with the grated cheese. (Serves 6).

Salade Bagration
Bagration Salad

8 artichoke hearts, cooked
4 stalks celery, blanched and chopped
1 cup ditalini or other small pasta, cooked al dente
½ cup smoked or pickled tongue, diced
4 Tbsp mayonnaise

2 chicken breasts, poached in chicken stock and then cut into dice
4 hard boiled eggs, quartered
watercress and tomato wedges for garnish
lemon juice

In a small bowl mix together the celery, ditalini, tongue and 2 Tbsp of the mayonnaise. With this mixture fill the artichoke hearts and place two on each plate. Surround the artichoke hearts with the diced chicken, hard boiled eggs, watercress and tomato wedges. Thin the remaining mayonnaise with lemon juice and drizzle this over the garnishes. Serve warm or cold. (Serves 4 as a first course).

Joachim Murat, 1767–1815
High Stakes

A general of the French armies under Napoleon, and later king of Naples, Joachim Murat was portrayed once in a newspaper column as "a man more dedicated to the pleasures of the casino than to his mistresses and more dedicated to them than to France." Napoleon himself observed that "Murat is a thief, of that I am certain, but he steals no more than any of my generals and at least has the good grace to spend the money he steals with great panache."

In 1800 Murat married Napoleon'a sister, Caroline, and four years later was made a marshal of France. In 1808 Napoleon made him the king of Naples, a title he held until 1815. During those years Murat maintained six different homes. His wife occupied a house in Arles, and in each of his other houses he installed one of his mistresses. He also maintained two apartments, one at place de Vosges in Paris and the other overlooking the harbor in Naples, and in both he entertained frequently—mainly married women. This sometimes caused the embarrassment of being challenged to a duel, but Murat, who never lost a duel, was a kind man and never did more than wound his opponents.

A notorious bon vivant, Murat spent long hours at the roulette tables of the casinos of Naples and Nice, where he is said to have lost a fortune. "The point is," he once wrote to one of his mistresses, "that it matters not whether I win or lose. After all, my access to the treasures of Naples and France guarantee that I will still die a wealthy man." His dining habits cost the French and Italian people far less than his gambling habits, because by 1798 he was so well known that restaurateurs stopped charging him for his meals. Years later, Sainte-Beuve wrote of Murat that "although some may admire him for his extravagances, it is unforgivable that he invariably ordered the wrong wines with his meals."

Upon Napoleon's downfall, Murat fled to Corsica from where he led an attempt to regain the throne of Naples.

The attempt failed and the former king was arrested by the forces of his rival, Ferdinand IV of Naples and was executed by firing squad in the small town of Pizzo.

The following dish was dedicated to Murat in 1813 by an Italian chef whose name has been lost to history.

Filets de Sole Murat
Fillets of Sole Murat

8 fillets of sole, cut into thin strips	¾ cup butter
4 large or 8 small artichoke hearts	¼ cup olive oil
½ lemon	8 thick tomato slices
juice of ½ lemon	salt and pepper
3 medium potatoes, peeled and cut into dice	2 eggs beaten lightly with 1 Tbsp water
	¼ cup parsley, chopped
	flour as required

If using fresh artichoke hearts, rub them with the lemon and place in about 1″ (2½ cm) boiling water to which the lemon juice has been added. Reduce the flame and simmer until the artichokes are about half cooked (about 8 minutes). Drain the artichoke hearts and cut into dice. (If using tinned hearts, simply drain them and cut them into dice).

In a small pot with lightly salted boiling water cook the potatoes until nearly tender and then drain well. In a heavy skillet melt ¼ cup of the butter and in this sauté the potatoes and artichoke dice until tender.

In a clean skillet heat the oil. Season the tomato slices with salt and pepper and sauté in the oil just until the tomatoes begin to brown. Remove with a slotted spoon and drain well.

Dip the sole fillets first in the eggs and then in the flour, coating well. In a heavy skillet melt ¼ cup more of the butter and in this sauté the fillets until golden brown on both sides. Transfer the fillets to a low flameproof casserole dish and mix in the potatoes and artichoke hearts. Sauté gently for 2–3 minutes and over all lay the tomato slices.

In a small saucepan melt the remaining butter. Raise the flame and, stirring constantly with a wooden spoon, cook until the butter is browned. Immediately before serving, sprinkle the fish with the parsley and then spoon over the hot browned butter. Serve immediately. (Serves 4).

The Duc d'Albufera, 1770–1826

To his Credit

Louis Gabriel Suchet, Duc d'Albufera, one of Napoleon's most distinguished generals and a marshal of France, became a hero after his victories at Oropeza and Valencia in 1812. On his return to Paris, everyone wanted to be known as a friend of the great general, and invitations came from every direction.

Bankers gave him unlimited credit, wine merchants sent him the best wines they had in their cellars, tailors competed for his business, and it was made known that the duke could eat in any restaurant in Paris without having to pay the bill. All of which suited Albufera, for despite his title and success, he was a man who had an enormous talent for spending money and none whatsoever for earning it. His 1814 report to the tax authorities comprised only one sentence that stated simply: "During the preceding year my expenses amounted to three million *livres* and my earnings were three thousand."

Neither his bankers nor his tailors seemed to mind that the duke never paid his bills, for he brought an enormous amount of business their way. One banker, Jacques Marny, was so anxious to capitalize on the Duke's name that he added the words "Personal Banker to the Duc d'Albufera" to his calling card. A tailor who supplied Albufera with part of his extensive wardrobe remarked that "the duke is a gentleman and I would never dream of asking him to pay his bills. I can happily report, however, that his friends honor their own debts promptly on the 15th of every month."

After the Duke's death, his house remained unoccupied for years, and in 1892 was bought by a certain Madame de Rœuf who converted it into a luxurious whorehouse. In the 1950s the building, at rue Serpente 12, in Paris' Latin Quarter, was converted into a reasonably priced two-star hotel, Le Serpent, popular today with American tourists.

The dish and sauces below were dedicated to Albufera by the great chef Carême.

Canetons à la d'Albufera
Duckling à la d'Albufera

2 very young ducklings, about
    1½ lb (675 gr) each
4 small apples, peeled
¾ cup butter
12 thin slices Prosciutto ham
1 bouquet garni made by tying
    together 4 sprigs of parsley,
    2 sprigs of tarragon and 1
    bay leaf

1 onion, studded with 2 whole
    cloves
½ cup Madeira or Port wine
½ cup Espagnole sauce (see
    p. 94)
6 oz (175 gr) very small
    mushrooms, peeled

In the cavity of each bird place an apple. Truss the birds well.

In a large flameproof casserole dish melt all but 1 Tbsp of the butter and over the melted butter lay the slices of ham. Place the ducklings on the ham slices, add the bouquet garni, the whole onion and the remaining apples and pour over the wine. Cover the casserole dish with aluminum foil that has been generously buttered on both sides and bring to the boil. Transfer at once to an oven that has been preheated to very hot. Immediately reduce the oven temperature to medium.

Cook for 20 minutes and then turn the birds, discarding the onion, apple, bouquet garni and aluminum foil. Let cook until the birds are done (about 35 minutes). During cooking baste the birds occasionally by spooning over the liquids in the casserole dish.

When the birds are done, drain them, remove the string with which they were tied, cut them in half and arrange on a serving platter. Garnish with the ham slices and set aside to keep warm. Discard the apples.

Skim off the excess fat from the liquids in the casserole dish, add the Espagnole sauce and remaining butter and mushrooms and heat through, stirring well and scraping the sides and bottom of the casserole dish with a wooden spatula. Spoon some of the sauce over the ducklings, place the remaining sauce in a small serving bowl and serve at once. (Serves 4).

Sauce Albufera

2 cups chicken stock
3 Tbsp liquids from tinned
    truffles or from soaking
    fresh truffles in warm water,
    strained
2 cups crème fraîche

3 Tbsp goose liver, poached
    and strained
2 Tbsp butter
1 tsp Madeira wine
salt to taste

In a saucepan bring the chicken stock and truffle liquids to a boil and cook until reduced by about one-third. Add the crème fraîche, reduce again by one-third and then thicken by stirring in the strained goose liver. Strain, add the butter and Madeira and correct the seasoning to taste. The sauce is ideal with roast goose, duck or chicken. (Yields about 2 cups).

The Duc d'Abrantes, 1771–1813
Catch of the Day

Few people have experienced as meteoric a rise to fame as Jean-Andoche Junot, a farmer's son who fought with Napoleon in all his campaigns and by the age of thirty attained the rank of general and was appointed Governor of Paris. The title Duc d'Abrantes was granted to him by the emperor after his victory in Portugal in 1807. According to his valet, Jean Boitelle, during his twenty year tenure Abrantes "had sixty-two different mistresses, embezzled over two hundred million *livres* and ate at least one magnificent meal every day."

A famous gourmand of his time, Abrantes entertained lavishly and was often to be found in the better known taverns and restaurants of Paris, where the patrons all knew that it would be "inappropriate" to present the governor with a bill. When it came to the table in his own home, Abrantes was fastidious, insisting that only the best and most expensive delicacies were to be served. Nearly every day he would accompany his servant to the market to oversee the purchase of the fruits and vegetables for the day.

Despite his flamboyant lifestyle, Abrantes was much admired by the common people of the city because he made sure that the price of bread, cheese and wine remained low. One of his habits in particular won the hearts of the Parisians: Every Thursday morning, regardless of how bad the weather might have been, he would leave his house at five A.M. From there, he made his way by foot to the banks of the Seine, where he would fish alongside the poorest people of the city for gudgeon, the delicate freshwater fish that were then so abundant in the river. The duke would catch eight fish, pack

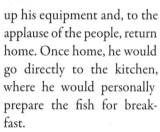

up his equipment and, to the applause of the people, return home. Once home, he would go directly to the kitchen, where he would personally prepare the fish for breakfast.

For six years the famed chef Richard was head of the Abrantes kitchens. In this capacity, the chef was in contact largely with the duke's wife, Laure, the Duchesse d'Abrantes, an author famous in her own right for her *mémoires*. As the duke was so often away from home, the duchess used Richard's services well, often entertaining such notables as the Empress Josephine and author Honoré de Balzac. Whether Richard named the following dish after the duke or duchess is not known, but both claimed that honor.

Tournedos à la d'Abrantes

4 tournedos
2 Tbsp olive oil
4 slices eggplant, ½″ (1 cm) thick, peeled
¼ cup + 2 tsp butter
4 medium potatoes, peeled and cut into ¼″ (½ cm) dice

salt and paprika to taste
¼ cup sweet red pepper, peeled and diced
3–4 Tbsp tomato puree
2 Tbsp onion, chopped coarsely

With 1 Tbsp of the oil brush both sides of the eggplant slices. Place the slices under a hot broiler and grill on both sides until nicely browned. Set aside to keep warm.

In a heavy skillet heat 2 Tbsp of the butter and in this sauté the potatoes until cooked through and nicely browned on the outside.

Season the tournedos to taste with salt and paprika. While the potatoes are cooking in one skillet, take another heavy skillet, heat together 2 Tbsp of butter with the remaining oil and in this sauté the tournedos over a high flame to ensure that they will be nicely done on the exterior but remain pink inside.

In a third skillet melt the remaining butter and in this sauté the red peppers briefly. Add 3 Tbsp of the tomato puree and heat through, adding the remaining tomato sauce if necessary to coat all of the red peppers.

When the tournedos are done, remove from the skillet and set aside to keep warm. In the same skillet sauté the onions until they just begin to brown. Add the red pepper and tomato sauce mixture and heat through.

To serve, place each tournedo on an eggplant slice, pour over the red pepper-onion mixture and garnish with the potatoes. (Serves 4).

Faisan à la d'Abrantes
Pheasant à la d'Abrantes

This dish was first devised by the monks at the Benedictine monastery at Alcántara in Spain. When Abrantes sacked the monastery in 1807 he found this recipe in the monks' manuscripts and sent it to his wife. Now carrying his name, the dish has become a well known classic of the French and Spanish kitchens.

1 young pheasant, aged and
    cleaned, with the wishbone
    and sternum removed
giblets of the pheasant, well
    cleaned
4–5 duck livers

12 walnut-sized black truffles
¼ cup olive oil
1 cup Oloroso Sherry
salt and freshly ground pepper
    to taste

Season the pheasant inside and out with salt and pepper to taste. Let stand for 30–40 minutes.

    In a small saucepan bring the Sherry to a bare simmer and drop in 4 of the truffles, letting them steep in the hot liquid for 30 minutes. Remove the truffles from the liquid and chop coarsely.

    Cut the giblets into small pieces and season with salt and pepper. In a small skillet heat half of the olive oil and in this sauté the giblets and livers until browned. Add the chopped truffles. With this mixture stuff the pheasant. Sew and truss the bird and place in a container with the Sherry and let stand in the refrigerator for 3 days to marinate, turning the bird once or twice daily.

    Transfer the pheasant to a baking dish, reserving the marinade separately. Pour the remaining oil over the bird and place in an oven that has been preheated to medium, basting after 10 minutes. Turn the bird after 15 minutes and cook, basting every ten minutes until the pheasant is golden brown, checking with the prongs of a fork to see if the flesh is tender (about 30 minutes cooking time in all).

    While the bird is in the oven, pour the marinade into a small saucepan and place the remaining whole truffles in this. Bring to a boil and let boil until the marinade is reduced by half. Add the marinade and the whole truffles to the baking dish with the pheasant about 10 minutes before the end of the cooking time. Serve the bird with the sauce and the whole truffles. (Serves 4).

Giuseppe Tortoni, 1775–1858

Melting Rendezvous

When the twenty-three-year-old Neapolitan ice-cream maker, Giuseppe Tortoni, came to Paris in 1798, he brought with him "an ancient and ailing mother, an ugly and bothersome wife, three ill-mannered children and a swaybacked horse who was the only member of my family who has any sympathies for my ambitions."

The first thing Tortoni did was to buy the nearly bankrupt Velloni's ice cream shop on rue de Rivoli. Soon the renamed Café Tortoni became one of Paris' most fashionable rendezvous. American author Washington Irving wrote that "never, in any single place, have I seen so many famous people simultaneously gathered for the purpose of satisfying their pleasures." It is no wonder that Irving was so impressed, for Tortoni's regular clients included diplomats Talleyrand and Metternich, Russian born banker Sir Basil Zaharoff, author Francois August Chateaubriand, the Duke of Mornay, the Baron de Rothschild, and Charles xiv, king of Sweden and Norway. So popular did the café become that when King Louis xviii wanted to reward a friend for his services, he tried to buy the café for him. Tortoni, wishing neither to sell nor to offend the king, set a price so outrageously high that even the king had to refuse the offer.

Tortoni, a superb inventor of ice cream dishes, was also a talented restaurateur and a shrewd psychologist. He supplied his male guests with lorgnettes, thus allowing them to appraise and comment on the attributes of the women walking by the café. Tortoni outlived his mother, his wife and his horse, and when he was eighty-nine years old wrote that "my children, although now adults, remain ill-mannered, and I fear for the fate of my little establishment once I am gone and it falls into their hands."

His fears proved groundless; his daughters, and later their children, maintained the ice cream parlor until 1900, when, during a particularly bad lightning storm, the building caught fire and burned to the ground. The popular meeting place never reopened, but several of Tortoni's inventions have lived on, and the two that follow are world famous.

Biscuit Tortoni

½ cup milk
2 cups sweet cream
1 cup macaroon cookies,
    crushed
5 Tbsp confectioners' sugar,
    sifted

small pinch of salt
1 tsp vanilla extract
Maraschino cherries for
    garnish
crushed toasted almonds
    (unsalted), for garnish

In a mixing bowl combine the milk and ½ cup of the sweet cream. Add the macaroons, sugar and salt and let stand, covered, for 1–2 hours.

Whip the remaining sweet cream until it is just stiff, taking care not to over-beat. Into this fold the macaroon mixture and the vanilla extract and then pour the mixture into 8 individual dessert glasses. Sprinkle each portion lightly with crushed nuts and on each place a maraschino cherry. Cover the glasses with plastic wrap and place in the freezer until frozen through. Transfer to the regular refrigeration compartment and discard the plastic wrap about 5 minutes prior to serving. (Serves 8).

Glacé aux Pêches Tortoni
Peach Ice Cream Tortoni

1 cup milk	¾ cup sugar
half cup whipping cream	1 tsp almond extract
1 vanilla bean about 2½″ (5 cm) long	¼ tsp salt
8 egg yolks	2 cups peaches, peeled, stoned and crushed

In a saucepan combine the cream, milk, and vanilla bean. Bring just to the point of boiling, immediately lower the flame and, stirring constantly, let simmer for 2–3 minutes. Remove the bean and reserve.

In a mixing bowl beat together the egg yolks and sugar until light. Gradually strain the hot cream and milk into the egg yolks, stirring briskly and then, into this mixture squeeze the seeds of the reserved vanilla bean. Transfer the mixture to the top of a double boiler and cook over but not in about 1″ (2½ cm) of simmering water until the mixture has the consistency of thick syrup. Remove from the heat, add the almond extract and then let cool, stirring occasionally.

Pour the mixture into chilled 2″ (5 cm) deep containers and cover with aluminum foil. Place in the freezer for 1 hour and then stir thoroughly. Return to the freezer for ½ hour more and then stir again. Pour the mixture into a large ring mold or bowl and mix in the crushed peaches. Return to the freezer, stir again after 30 more minutes and then let freeze solid. (Yields about 2 quarts [2 liters]).

Madame Récamier, 1777–1849

Salon's Food

In 1792, Jeanne Françoise Julie Adélaïde Bernard, age fifteen, was married to the wealthy banker Jacques Récamier and soon her salon became the most fashionable in Paris. She attracted some of the most influential political and literary figures of the time, from Klemens von Metternich and Jean-Baptiste Bernadotte to Victor Hugo, Alexis de Tocqueville, Alfred de Musset and Benjamin Constant. Although many men fell in love with her, it is probable that she never had any but platonic attachments, even with her husband, until she met and became attached to the writer and statesman François-René Chateaubriand in 1817. She remained devoted to him until his death in 1848, and died herself a year later.

The celebrated society beauty met Napoleon Bonaparte only once, when he was First Consul, at the home of his brother Lucien Bonaparte. Since they were not seated together, they hardly exchanged a word. Later, she came to despise Napoleon, not only because he declined to help her husband when he was financially ruined but also because to her he represented the epitome of misogynism. She objected, for example, to the Code Napoleon, which dictated that wives belong to their husbands in "heart and soul", could not inherit property, and were declared unfit under the law.

Récamier's salon became a fortress of opposition to Napoleon, but she herself found more subtle and even amusing ways to express her free spirit. From her boudoir one evening she decreed that it would always be April. On another occasion she declared that the sun would always shine on Tuesdays and, if on the day following Monday the sun did not shine, it would simply be Wednesday. On the occasion of one of her journeys to Coppet in Swizerland to meet her friend Madame de Stahl, a fierce opponent of Napoleon, she was informed by Napoleon's Minister of Police, Joseph Fouché, that she was perfectly at liberty to go to Switzerland, but that she could not return to Paris. "Ah, Monseigneur! A great man may be pardoned for the weakness of loving women, but not for fearing them," was her answer. She returned to Paris only on Napoleon's downfall in 1815.

As much as she was involved with the rights of women, Madame Récamier was no less dedicated to dining well, believing that "without good food there can be no good life." Although her entertaining at home was generally limited to groups of four, five or six visitors, she would not hesitate to devote sixteen hours to preparing a meal "so delicious that five years from now no one will remember   what we talked about this evening but everyone will remember
with great fondness everything upon which
they dined."

The first recipe below was
devised by Madame Récamier
on the occasion of her fiftieth birthday. The second, a
simple but superb dessert,
was dedicated to her by
Chevrier, a well known maitre d'hotel.

Flan au Fromage Juliette Récamier
Cheese Flan à la Juliette Récamier

FOR THE PASTRY:

2¼ cups flour, sifted
1 egg
10 Tbsp butter

2 Tbsp sugar
¾ tsp salt

FOR THE CREAM:

2¼ cups milk
½ tsp vanilla extract
½ cup flour, sifted

¼ tsp salt
1 Tbsp butter, softened
4 eggs

FOR THE CHEESE FLAN:

½ lb (225 gr) beef bone marrow,
    cut in thin slices
2 cups veal stock, boiled down
    to 1 cup
About ¾ cup dry white wine,
    as required
2 Tbsp shallots or green parts
    of green onions, chopped

2 Tbsp parsley, chopped
salt, pepper and nutmeg to
    taste
3 Tbsp butter
6 eggs
6 Tbsp Gruyere cheese, grated

Prepare the pastry: On a flat working board spread the flour in a circle and in the centre make a well. Into this well place the egg, butter, sugar, salt and ⅓ cup of water. Mix these ingredients together and then gradually work them into the flour. When the mixture is smooth knead the mixture two times only and then roll the dough into a ball. Wrap the dough in a lightly dampened cloth and keep in a cool place until ready for use. The dough should be prepared 2–3 hours before use and should not be handled excessively.

Prepare the cream: In a saucepan mix together the milk and vanilla and bring just to the boil. In a separate heavy saucepan combine the flour, salt, butter and eggs and work together with a wooden spoon. Add the milk and vanilla mixture, stir, place over a medium flame and bring again to the boil. Stirring constantly, let boil for 2–3 minutes. Pour into a preheated bowl and let cool, stirring occasionally.

Prepare the flan filling: Place the marrow in a flat pan and pour over the veal stock. Let stand for 15 minutes and drain. Pour over just enough white wine to cover, add the shallots and parsley, and cook over a medium flame until the moisture has almost disappeared. Season to taste with salt, pepper and nutmeg, and crush the marrow with a fork.

Roll out the pastry and line a pie case that has been lightly buttered and floured. Spread the marrow on the bottom of the case and then fill half full with the cream. Bake in a medium oven for 20–25 minutes.

While the flan is baking, melt the butter in a heavy skillet. Beat the eggs lightly together with 4 Tbsp of the grated cheese, pour into the skillet and scramble the eggs.

When the flan is baked, fill it with the scrambled eggs, sprinkle over the remaining cheese and place under a hot grill to brown rapidly. Serve at once. (Serves 4).

Pêches Madame Récamier
Peaches à la Madame Récamier

5 cups sugar	8 egg yolks
3½ tsp vanilla extract	pinch of salt
4 peaches, pitted, halved and peeled	2¼ cups milk, boiled

In a saucepan bring 2 cups of water to the boil and in this dissolve 4 cups of the sugar. Strain and filter this syrup into the top of a double boiler, add 3 tsp of the vanilla extract and place over but not in boiling water. Place the peaches, cut side down, in the syrup, cover and cook gently for 8–10 minutes. Drain the peaches and transfer to small dessert plates.

In the top of a double boiler, over but not in simmering water, blend together the egg yolks, remaining sugar and salt until the syrup forms a ribbon when the spatula is lifted from the pan. Gradually add

the boiled milk which has been flavored with the remaining vanilla extract. Pour the custard through a fine sieve and then spoon the custard over the peaches. Serve immediately. (Serves 4).

Count Nesselrode, 1780–1862

A Russian in Paris

Aprominent Russian statesman, Count Karl Robert Nesselrode served Czar Alexander I as state secretary, foreign minister and chancellor, and for forty years until his death was the guiding force behind Russian policy. Nesselrode had great influence during that period, when French language, the fashions of Paris, and the grand cuisine of France were de rigueur among Russian aristocrats. In fact, having a French chef was as important to social success as having the right connections with the royal family.

The extraordinarily wealthy Nesselrode enjoyed his many trips to Paris. During the day he was frequently to be found at the stock exchange, and at nights he was invariably entertaining friends, either in his luxurious eighteen room apartment or at the best restaurants of the city. On one occasion, during a particularly bad day at the stock exchange, Nesselrode lost five million rubles, the equivalent then of four million dollars. That evening, when a friend offered his condolences, Nesselrode merely shrugged, waved his hand in the air and replied: "Not to worry, my friend. There is an additional fifty million that are left to lose if I choose to do it again tomorrow."

Nesselrode, who once wrote that "there are only two things

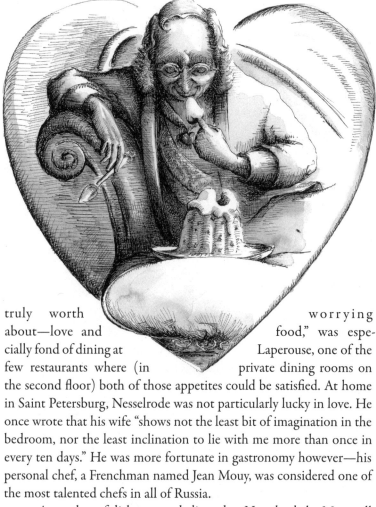

truly worth   worrying about—love and   food," was espe-cially fond of dining at   Laperouse, one of the few restaurants where (in   private dining rooms on the second floor) both of those appetites could be satisfied. At home in Saint Petersburg, Nesselrode was not particularly lucky in love. He once wrote that his wife "shows not the least bit of imagination in the bedroom, nor the least inclination to lie with me more than once in every ten days." He was more fortunate in gastronomy however—his personal chef, a Frenchman named Jean Mouy, was considered one of the most talented chefs in all of Russia.

A number of dishes were dedicated to Nesselrode by Mouy, all containing chestnuts. The most famous of these are a pudding and an ice cream bombe, both of which are still offered regularly in Laperouse, at 51 quai des Grands-Augustins in Paris. One may still dine in the small, private dining rooms, each furnished with a chaise-longue from which one can still see the entwined hearts, names and dates that courtesans scratched on the mirrors with their diamonds. Gone, however, are the bidets that were disguised as flower vases.

Pouding Nesselrode
Nesselrode Pudding

40 chestnuts, blanched and
    peeled
2 cups water
2 cups sugar
1 vanilla bean, split lengthwise
3¾ cups whipping cream
12 egg yolks
½ cup + 1 Tbsp Maraschino
    liqueur

1 oz candied lemon peel,
    chopped finely
2 oz (60 gr) each currants and
    raisins
3 egg whites
sweetened whipped cream
chopped candied lemon peel for
    decorating

In a saucepan bring the water to a boil and into this mix the sugar and add the vanilla bean. Stir regularly with a wooden spoon until a smooth, moderately thick syrup is formed (about 10 minutes). Discard the vanilla bean.

With a wooden mallet crush the chestnuts and then mix in 2 Tbsp of the sugar syrup. Pass the chestnuts through a sieve into a large ovenproof bowl, and then add and mix in the remaining syrup.

In a bowl, mix together 2½ cups of the whipping cream and the egg yolks. Place the bowl over a pan of simmering water on a gentle flame and heat through, stirring constantly. Remove from the heat just as the mixture comes to a boil. Pass the mixture through a sieve into a clean bowl and set aside to cool. When the mixture is cool add ½ cup of the Maraschino liqueur, cover and transfer to the refrigerator for 10–12 hours.

While the pudding is cooling place the lemon peel, currants and raisins in a bowl and spoon over the remaining Maraschino liqueur and toss gently. Set aside to marinate for 8–12 hours, stirring occasionally.

Add the marinated fruits to the chilled chestnut mixture.

Whip the remaining sweet cream until fluffy but not stiff. In a separate bowl whisk the egg whites until stiff peaks form. Fold the whipped cream and beaten egg whites into the chestnut mixture, pour into a mold and transfer, covered, to the freezer until firm but not quite frozen.

Dip the mold into a large bowl of warm water for 2–3 seconds and then carefully turn out the pudding from the mould onto a serving plate. Decorate with candied lemon peel and whipped cream and serve. (Serves 6–8).

Bombe Nesselrode

1½ cups glazed chestnuts
3 Tbsp kirsch or vishniac
About 4 cups vanilla ice cream,
    softened but not melted

7 cups sugar
32 egg yolks
2 tsp vanilla extract
3 cups sweet cream, beaten stiff

Rub the chestnuts through a fine sieve and place them in a small bowl. Pour over the kirsch liqueur and let them soak for 1–2 hours, stirring every 15 minutes.

Line a 10 cup bombe mold or glass bowl with the vanilla ice cream and place in the freezer until the ice cream is completely solidified.

In a saucepan dissolve the sugar in 4 cups of water. Bring to a rapid boil, strain and filter. In the top of a large double boiler over but not in hot water, combine the syrup and egg yolks, stirring regularly with a wire whisk. When the mixture attains the consistency of sweet cream pour it into a bowl. Add the vanilla extract and continue to stir until the mixture is completely cool. Add the pureed chestnuts to the mixture and then fold in the whipped cream. Place the mixture in a glass or ceramic container, cover and refrigerate for 4–5 hours. With this mixture fill the center of the bombe. Cover with plastic wrap and return to the freezer until the mixture is solid throughout (2–3 hours).

Dip the mold or bowl in a large bowl of hot water for a few second. Place a chilled serving plate on top of the mold and invert quickly. (Serves 10–12).

Jean Paul Very, 1780–1848
Ménage à Quatre

W hen Jean Paul Very came to Paris in 1798, he had relatively little baggage. Recording his travels in a diary, he listed his paraphernalia as "two shirts, an extra pair of trousers, a small dog, a troublesome orange-colored cat and a wife two years younger than myself." Two days after his arrival, Very started work as a kitchen boy at the famous Restaurant Meot. Three days later he made the acquaintance of Geraud-Christophe-Michel Duroc, the Duc de Frioul, who was a regular customer at the restaurant.

Duroc took a liking to the young man and, realizing how badly he needed money, offered to employ Very's wife, Mathilde, in his household. Before long Duroc had become Mathilde's lover, while Very was spending his free hours in the bedroom of the Duchesse de Frioul, Duroc's wife. This set up proved favorable to all parties involved for many years to come. When Very, who turned out to be a remarkable chef, aspired to open a restaurant at the Tuileries palace, Duroc gave him financial backing and encouraged his own friends to go there. By 1808 Very was so well established that he could afford to buy three arcades at the Palais-Royal, where he moved his restaurant.

By this time Duroc had become a general in Napoleon's army, and

brought the Emperor to visit Very's restaurant. Napoleon, impressed, proclaimed that "the decor was impeccable, the service perfect, the cuisine exquisite"; quite a compliment from a man who never devoted more than fifteen minutes to a meal.

The following dishes were dedicated by Very in gratitude to his friend and benefactor.

Entrecôte Duroc

FOR THE STEAKS:

4 entrecote steaks, trimmed and lightly flattened
¾ lb (350 gr) small potatoes
6 Tbsp butter

1 Tbsp olive oil
1–2 Tbsp tarragon, chopped
salt and pepper to taste

FOR THE CHASSEUR SAUCE:

½ cup butter
2 cups mushrooms, chopped
2 Tbsp white parts of spring onions, chopped finely
½ cup dry white wine
1 cup beef or veal stock boiled down to half

½ cup tomato sauce
1 tsp each fresh parsley and chervil, chopped
2 tsp fresh tarragon, chopped
salt to taste

In a saucepan with lightly salted water boil the potatoes until just tender. Drain and peel. In a skillet heat ¼ cup of the butter and in this sauté the potatoes, shaking the pan often until the potatoes are nicely browned. Set aside to keep warm.

Season the steaks with salt and pepper. In a clean heavy skillet heat together the olive oil and remaining butter and in this sauté the steaks, browning then nicely on both sides. Transfer the steaks to a serving plate and set aside to keep warm.

Prepare the chasseur sauce: In the skillet in which the steaks were sautéed melt 2 Tbsp of the butter and in this sauté the mushrooms. When the mushrooms are nearly cooked season to taste with salt and add the spring onions. When the mushrooms are cooked through add the white wine, boil down by half and stir in the beef stock and tomato sauce. Let boil for about 1 minute, remove from the flame, add the remaining butter, parsley, chervil and 1 tsp of the tarragon and stir well.

To serve, surround the steaks with the potatoes and sprinkle a few teaspoons of the sauce over the meat. Sprinkle the meat with the tarragon and serve the remaining sauce separately. (Serves 4).

Note: This recipe can also be made using veal steaks, fillets mignons or lamb chops.

Poulet Duroc
Chicken à la Duroc

2 small chickens, about 4½ lb (2 kilos) in all, cut in convenient serving pieces
1 lb (450 gr) very small potatoes
¾ cup butter
12 small tomatoes, peeled
2 Tbsp olive oil
1 cup mushrooms, sliced
½ cup white wine
white parts of 6 spring onions, chopped
1 cup veal stock, boiled until reduced by half
2 Tbsp tomato sauce
1 Tbsp brandy
2 Tbsp parsley, chopped
½ Tbsp each chervil and tarragon, chopped
salt and pepper to taste

In a saucepan with lightly salted water boil the potatoes until just tender. Drain and peel. In a skillet heat ¼ cup of the butter and in this sauté the potatoes, shaking the pan often until the potatoes are nicely browned. With a slotted spoon remove the potatoes and set aside to keep warm.

In the same skillet, adding butter if necessary, sauté the tomatoes gently until tender. Set aside to keep warm.

In a clean, large heavy skillet heat together the oil and 2 Tbsp of the butter. Season the chicken pieces with salt and pepper and sauté them in the skillet. When the chicken is about ¾ cooked (about 20–25 minutes) add the mushrooms and continue to sauté, stirring regularly. When cooked, remove the chicken pieces with a slotted spoon and place on a preheated serving platter. Spoon the mushrooms over the chicken pieces.

To the pan juices add the wine and spring onions and boil down to less than half the original quantity. Add the veal stock and tomato sauce, boil for 30–40 seconds, and then add the brandy, the parsley, the chervil and the tarragon. To serve garnish the chicken with the potatoes and tomatoes, spoon over some of the sauce and serve the remaining sauce separately. (Serves 6–8).

Daniel-François-Esprit Auber, 1782–1871

Music of Dining

Described once by Lillie Moulton, wife of a well-known American banker, as "a short, dapper little man, with such a refined and clever face," Daniel-François-Esprit Auber, who composed fifty operas and over two hundred pieces for strings, was much admired by the composers of his time. Once, when he complemented Georges Bizet on his work, Bizet replied: "I accept your praise but do not reciprocate it." Auber is said to have grimaced—until Bizet explained that a private in the army may receive the praise of a marshal of France, but does not return it. The two became fast friends, although in general Auber preferred the company of authors and literary critics. Even though he was forty years older than the eldest of the Goncourt Brothers, he was an integral part of their social circle. He was also friendly with Victor Hugo and the critic Charles Augustin Sainte-Beuve, with whom he would often enjoy the bouillabaisse at the luxurious Maison Dorée. Auber also enjoyed dining at Magny, a popular Left Bank restaurant of the nineteenth century. In 1842 he was appointed to the faculty of the Paris Conservatory, a post he retained until his death at the age of eighty-nine. Several days before his death, commenting on his advancing age, he observed with a sigh that "aging seems to be the only available way to live a long life."

Although many of his works are now considered second-rate, Auber's name is not forgotten; in addition to a Metro station in Paris, there are streets that carry his name in twenty-six cities and towns. Even his face remains well known, since it is immortalized in music conservatories throughout France.

Auber's wife rarely accompanied him when he dined out. She wrote once that she "preferred the peace and quiet of her Paris apartment to the noise and sometimes pompous intellectuality" of her husband's friends. The couple did have the custom, however, on certain holidays, of inviting a small group of family and friends to dine with them at the fashionable Maison Dorée. The chefs there and at other restaurants knew Auber, and respected his taste in food, as a result of which at least twelve well-known dishes have been named after him. The following, probably the most famous, was dedicated to him by one of the chefs at the Maison Dorée when the Aubers dined there in 1860.

Œufs Auber
Eggs Auber

½ lb (225 gr) bacon, in thin slices

5 oz (150 gr) each chicken and lean veal, both cooked and chopped

6 Tbsp brandy

1 raw egg

½ tsp black pepper

1 tsp paprika

½ tsp salt

2–3 oz (60–85 gr) truffles, chopped

4 large tomatoes

2 oz (60 gr) mushrooms, sliced very thinly

1½ cups Sherry wine

¼ cup chicken stock

1 tsp tomato puree

½ tsp dried oregano

8 eggs, poached just before ready to serve

In a skillet fry the bacon slices until crisp. Drain on paper towels, and then chop them.

In a food processor or blender, blend together the chopped

bacon, chicken and veal. To the mixture add the brandy, raw egg, pepper, ½ tsp of the paprika and ½ tsp of salt. Rub the mixture through a sieve, add the truffles and mix together thoroughly. Place in an oven that has been heated to low just until the mixture has been heated through and then reduce the oven temperature to its minimum, just to keep the mixture warm.

With a sharp knife cut a cross in the top of each of the tomatoes. Plunge the tomatoes into boiling water for 30 seconds, run them under cold water, drain them and remove the skins. Cut the tomatoes in half and scoop the seeds and pulp, leaving the halves hollow. Turn the halves upside down and let drain for 15–20 minutes.

Sprinkle the mushrooms with salt. In a small saucepan bring the Sherry to the boil and to this add the mushrooms. Reduce to a gentle simmer and cook for 30 minutes. Drain and set aside to keep warm

In a clean saucepan heat the chicken stock and in this dissolve the tomato paste, oregano and remaining paprika. Heat and stir regularly until the mixture thickens somewhat.

With the chicken, veal and bacon mixture fill the tomato shells and on each half place one of the poached eggs. Spoon over the thickened chicken stock, sprinkle over the cooked mushrooms and serve at once. (Serves 8 as a first course or 4 as a luncheon dish).

Marie-Antoine Carême, 1784–1833
The Chef of Chefs

Marie-Antoine Carême, who was born to parents so poor that they abandoned him in the streets of Paris when he was ten years old, rose to culinary and social heights attained by no chef before or after him, and was acknowledged even in his lifetime as the founder of French haute cuisine. At the age of thirteen he was working in a restaurant frequented mostly by sailors and whores. There he met the famed Parisian *pâtissier*, Sylvain Bailly, who took him on as an apprentice. In his later years, Bailly liked to boast that "even though I was a great baker, the most important thing I ever did was to rescue Carême from that terrible place."

Bailly encouraged his young protégé to spend long hours at the national library to study the architecture of Greece and Rome in order to find inspiration for the design of his cakes. Consequently, Carême acquired a reputation for his elaborate confections, those marvelous marzipan and sugar centerpiece constructions that were then essential at any grand dinner. Later he carried his affection for architecture to main courses, sculpting picturesque ruins with lard.

Carême spent twelve years as chef to French diplomat and gourmet Charles Maurice de Talleyrand, who challenged his chef to create a whole year's menus without repeating any dishes, and using only seasonal ingredients. Young Carême met the challenge and through doing so became one of France's most accomplished cuisiniers. In 1815 he crossed the channel to England, where for two years he was chef to the Prince Regent, later King George IV, who promised him a castle of his own if he would stay on. Carême, who loathed the fog of London, moved on to Saint Petersburg as chef to Czar Alexander I, who acknowledged his genius by saying: "He taught us to eat."

Upon his return to France, Carême served as a chef to Baron de Rothschild, with whom he stayed for seven years, dividing his time between cooking, and writing *L'art de la Cuisine Française*, an exhaustive survey of classic French cuisine in the nineteenth century. This five volume work that codifies the principles, philosophy and standards of classic cuisine is popular among chefs even today, and many of them make it their habit to read a few pages every night before retiring. The last two volumes were completed after Carême's death by Armand Plumerey, a close friend and colleague.

Carême is credited with numerous sauces, dishes and kitchen utensils, among them the *toque*—the classic chef's hat. It was he who classified all sauces into groups based on the four mother sauces which are the basics of French haute cuisine, and to him we owe the division between fish, poultry and meat, a principle which prevails to this day in all modern cuisines. Carême died just short of his fiftieth birthday, burnt, as his friend, author Laurent Tailhade wrote, "by the flame of his genius and the charcoal of the roasting spit." His last moments were spent dictating notes to his daughter on how to prepare a raspberry sauce for a partridge. He also left behind a legacy that made him forever the "chef of kings and the king of chefs."

Carême's recipes are rarely used today, as most of them are so intricate that they require a full day in the kitchen. The first recipe that follows was dedicated to Carême by the famed chef Georges Auguste Escoffier when he was in charge of the kitchens at the Grand Hotel in Monte Carlo, and the second was invented by Carême during his stay in Russia and was dedicated to his employer Czar Alexander Romanoff. Among others of Carême's recipes found in this book are Potage Apicius, Duckling Albufera, Potage Bagration and Consommé Brillat-Savarin.

Œufs Carême
Eggs Carême

8 eggs
½ lb (225 gr) calf or veal
    sweetbreads
2 Tbsp red or white wine
    vinegar
1¼ cups butter

1 cup mushrooms, diced
1 recipe for Allemande sauce
    (See p. 98)
1 tsp lemon juice
8 large artichoke hearts
8 slices pickled tongue

Soak the sweetbreads in cold water for 1 hour, changing the water several times. Transfer to a saucepan and add cold water to cover. Add the vinegar, bring slowly to the boil and then simmer, uncovered for 3–4 minutes. Plunge the sweetbreads into cold water, drain, let cool and cut into small dice.

In a skillet melt 3 Tbsp of the butter and in this gently sauté the mushrooms, taking care not to let them brown. Drain the excess butter. In a mixing bowl combine the mushrooms, sweetbreads and just enough of the Allemande sauce to moisten the mixture.

To a saucepan containing 1″ (2½ cm) of boiling water, add the lemon juice and in this simmer the artichoke hearts for 15 minutes. In a clean skillet melt the remaining butter and in this cook the artichoke hearts, turning gently several times, until they are tender (4–5 minutes). Drain the butter.

Cut the tongue slices into rounds just a bit smaller than the artichoke hearts.

Poach the eggs and place one egg in the hollow of each artichoke heart. Over this spoon the sweetbread mixture, and then spoon over the remaining Allemande sauce. Over each egg lay a slice of the tongue. (Serves 4 or 8 as a first course).

Fraises Romanoff
Strawberries Romanoff

Carême's original recipe called for Cointreau liqueur, but in France today many use Curacao, and Americans add vanilla ice cream and use Grand Marnier liqueur.

2–3 cups strawberries, washed, hulled and halved

6 Tbsp sugar

1 cup whipping cream

¼ cup Cointreau

Sprinkle the strawberries with 4 Tbsp of the sugar and chill for 2–3 hours in the refrigerator. Immediately before serving mix the remaining sugar with the whipping cream and beat the cream until stiff. Fold the liqueur into the stiff whipped cream and then fold in the strawberries. (Serves 4–6).

Gioacchino Antonio Rossini, 1792–1868

In a Lighter Mood

With the downfall of Napoleon in 1815, Europeans had grown tired of war and were ready to sit back and enjoy life. Nothing typified the new, lighter mood of the period more than the operas of Gioacchino Antonio Rossini.

A native of Pesaro, Italy, Rossini traveled extensively, and at various times made his home in Bologna, Florence and Paris. Once, in a letter to a friend, he wrote: "I travel not so much for the sake of my music as for that of my stomach." By the time he was eighteen, Rossini had written his first opera. Between 1813 and 1823 he produced twenty-five more, and claimed to have made the acquaintance of every important chef on the continent. He was a close friend of the great chef Antonin Carême, who was known to send Rossini game pâté, the maestro reciprocating by writing an aria for his friend.

In Paris, Rossini's favorite dish was turkey stuffed with truffles, a very fashionable dish of the period. As myth goes, Rossini wept only three times in his life: over the fiasco of his first opera, upon listening to Paganini play the violin, and when a turkey stuffed with truffles fell overboard during a boating outing.

After the success of *Guillaume Tell* in Paris in 1829, when Rossini

was only thirty-seven, he retired and enjoyed the remaining forty years of his life composing hardly at all and living for the companionship of his friends, witty conversation and excellent dining in such restaurants as the Tour d'Argent, Bonfinger, the Café des Anglais, Maison Dorée, Lucas and Marguery. It was his habit upon entering his favorite restaurants to shake the hands of the maitre d'hotel, the wine steward and each of the waiters, then to go to the kitchen to greet the chef and only then to ceremoniously take his place. In each of these restaurants he had a table reserved exclusively for him.

Story has it that the world famous dish Tournedos Rossini originated at the Café Anglais in Paris, when Rossini, anxious to oversee the preparation of his meal, insisted that the chef cook it in the diningroom next to his table. When the chef objected, the maestro replied, *"Et alors, tournez le dos."* ("So, turn your back.") However, other evidence suggests that this recipe, as well as the recipe for Eggs Rossini, were actually dedicated to Rossini by Casimir Moisson, the great chef of Maison Dorée.

Œufs Rossini
Eggs Rossini

FOR THE SAUCE:
1½ Tbsp Madeira wine	1¼ cups veal stock
¾ Tbsp corn flour	salt and pepper to taste

FOR THE EGGS:
8 eggs	3–4 truffles, sliced very thinly
¼ cup butter	salt and pepper to taste
½ lb (225 gr) goose liver, sliced	

Make the sauce: In a small bowl mix the Madeira and corn flour to make a paste. Bring the stock to a boil and gradually whisk the paste into the hot stock. Return to the boil, whisking constantly, and then simmer until thick enough to coat the back of a spoon. Season to taste with salt and pepper and then strain through a fine strainer.

Prepare the dish: In a skillet melt 3 Tbsp of the butter and in this sauté the goose liver. In a separate skillet, melt the remaining butter and in this toss the truffles, sautéing for 1–2 minutes.

Poach the eggs and season lightly with salt and pepper. Place each egg on a slice of the goose liver, top with truffle slices and cover with the sauce. (Serves 2 or 4).

Tournedos Rossini

4 slices white bread, without
    crusts and trimmed to the
    size of the tournedos
6 Tbsp butter
4 slices goose liver
4 tournedos
salt and pepper to taste
2 Tbsp olive oil
3 cloves garlic, sliced thinly

1 Tbsp Port
1 Tbsp Cognac
About ½ cup *demi-glace* or
    Espagnole sauce (see p. 94)
2 truffles, sliced

In a small skillet melt 2 Tbsp of the butter and in this gently sauté the goose liver slices. Set aside to keep warm.

In a separate small skillet melt 2 Tbsp of butter and in this fry the white bread slices until nicely browned on both sides.

Season the tournedos with salt and pepper. In a skillet, heat together the remaining butter and the olive oil and in this sauté the garlic just until it begins to brown. With a slotted spoon remove and discard the garlic. Place the tournedos in the skillet and cook over a high flame so that the meat is nicely browned on the exterior and pink on the inside. Place each tournedo on a toasted bread slice.

In the skillet in which the meat was fried briefly sauté the truffles. On each tournedo lay a slice of the goose liver and over these distribute the truffles. Heat the pan juices, add the Port and Cognac, scraping the skillet well with a wooden spoon and then add the Espagnole sauce, stirring together well. Pour a small amount of the sauce over the meat and serve immediately. Serve the remaining sauce separately. (Serves 4).

Alexandre Dumas, 1802–1870

Culinary Fictions

K nown during his lifetime as "the King of Paris", Alexandre Dumas is remembered today primarily for his historical novels *Les Trois Mousquetaires* and *Le Comte De Monte-Cristo*. However, his rich legacy embraces over three hundred volumes of novels, plays, travel journals and memoirs, which earned him a huge fortune and even greater fame.

Dumas was a cook as well as a gourmet, and his *Dictionnaire de Cuisine*, published posthumously in 1873, is a marvelous compendium of French dining habits throughout history. He recounts, for example, how Napoleon's chancellor, Jean-Jacques Cambacérès, during one of his grand dinners, directed his servants to pretend to stumble and drop the pièce de résistance, a rare eighty kilogram sturgeon from the Caspian Sea. While the guests were still gasping at their loss, their prodigal host clapped his hands and a second, even larger sturgeon was carried in. That the book is outrageously inaccurate only adds to its charm, as Dumas never lets on whether he himself believes the myths he perpetuates.

Among those myths is a tale of how the Romans drove ducks across the Alps for their feasts (a task that would have taken years), how Caribbean natives feed "almost exclusively" on crabs, and how one can

make a pie from the stomach of a young shark (he does add the comment that he had never eaten it and has "no wish to do so.") To prove how playful he could be, this man who so adored wine devotes two full pages to rejecting its merits and praising the virtues of water.

Dumas lived much as his adventurous protagonists did, participating in the revolution of 1830, becoming a captain in the National Guard, contracting cholera during the 1832 epidemic, and with the money earned from his books, erecting the magnificent Château de Monte-Cristo near Paris. He was alleged to have had dozens of children by his numerous mistresses, but acknowledged only three, among them the playwright Alexandre Dumas fils. Dumas spent his fortune so rapidly that in 1851 he had to flee from his creditors to Brussels in order to avoid a debtor's jail sentence. He also traveled to Russia and Italy, where he supported Garibaldi. Upon his return to Paris in 1864, restaurateurs welcomed him, even though it was well known that he would never pay his bills.

In a letter to a friend, Dumas wrote: "It is my habit each week to dine at restaurants three times, to take dinner at the home of friends twice, to dine alone at home once and, every Tuesday, to entertain five or six people in my home." Although he was most famous for the salads he served at those Tuesday dinners, his name is today associated with a steak dish and a soup, those probably devised and dedicated to Dumas by one of the sous-chefs at Magny, where he dined frequently.

Steak Dumas

4 entrecote steaks, trimmed and lightly flattened
about 1½ cups veal or beef stock
12 thin slices of beef marrow
about ¾ cup butter
½ cup dry white wine
3 Tbsp shallots, chopped
2 Tbsp parsley, chopped
salt and pepper to taste

In a saucepan bring 1 cup of stock to the boil. Lower the flame immediately so that the liquid is barely simmering and in this poach the marrow for 2–3 minutes. Drain.

Season the steaks with salt and pepper. In a heavy skillet melt

2–3 Tbsp of the butter and in this sauté the steaks briefly on both sides. Transfer the steaks to a preheated serving platter and set aside to keep warm.

Make a pan gravy by adding the white wine and shallots to the liquids already in the skillet. Scrape the pan and stir well while boiling down the liquids to ⅓ of their original volume. Add the remaining veal stock, bring to the boil and boil for 1 minute. Add ½ cup of butter and season to taste. To serve, place 3 slices of the bone marrow on each steak, season generously with coarsely ground black pepper and sprinkle over the chopped parsley. Spoon over the pan gravy and serve immediately. (Serves 4).

Crème d'Asperges à la Dumas
Cream of Asparagus Soup à la Dumas

FOR THE SOUP:

1 lb (450 gr) fresh green asparagus, well washed
¾ cups milk
½ quarts (1½ liters) chicken stock
½ cup celery, chopped

¼ cup onion, chopped
about ¼ cup butter
3 Tbsp flour
¼ cup sweet cream
salt, white pepper and paprika to taste

FOR THE LOBSTER MOUSSE:

Meat of one 1½–1¾ lb (675–800 gr) lobster, cooked and cooled
3 oz (85 gr) of scallops (coquilles Saint Jacques)

½ tsp sea salt
½ cup sweet cream
½ tsp chives, snipped
½ tsp lobster roe (optional)

To prepare the mousse: Using a mortar and pestle or a food processor, puree the lobster meat together with the scallops and salt. Mixing constantly or with the motor running, add the sweet cream in a steady stream and blend well, but take care not to over process as the mixture will separate.

Force the mousse through a fine strainer into a bowl, stir in the chives and lobster roe, transfer to a round container, cover and chill for between 4–8 hours.

To prepare the soup: Separate the asparagus tips from the rest of the stalks and simmer them in ½ cup of the milk until the tips are tender (about 8–10 minutes). Take care not to let the mixture boil during cooking.

Cut the stalks of the asparagus into pieces and place them in a saucepan with the stock, celery and onion. Cover the saucepan, simmer for about ½ hour and then rub through a sieve.

Melt the butter and stir in the flour, stirring until well blended. To this slowly add the cream, remaining milk and asparagus puree. Heat in a double boiler over hot water and add the asparagus tips.

Immediately before serving, season to taste with salt, pepper and paprika. Ladle the soup into individual soup bowls. Divide the lobster mousse into equal portions and place one portion in the center of each soup bowl. (Serves 4–6).

Hector Berlioz, 1803–1869

Café Notes

Suffering from mood swings that ranged from euphoria to despair, and desperately craving social acceptance, Hector Berlioz was not popular among other composers. During his lifetime, he was far better known as a literary critic, where his talents, notably for the *Journal des Débates* and *Gazette Musicale*, proved a more dependable source of income than his musical output. He became a powerful figure in literary circles, and was frequently to be found holding court in the various restaurants of Paris, amusing his friends with his sharp wit and cutting tongue.

Berlioz especially enjoyed passing time in those cafés and restaurants where the owners would allow him to put together two or three tables, cover them with his musical notepaper, and work on his compositions. In his memoirs he wrote: "To my great joy, two of my operas [*Benvenuto Cellini* and *Beatrice and Benedict*] were born, grew to maturation and made their way to paper, over hot chocolate and cakes at the Café de Paris." When this establishment closed in 1858, Berlioz transferred his affections to the then newly opened Bonfinger, where his favorite dish was lobster mayonnaise.

He was also a regular client at Magny, feasting there with George

Sand, Charles Augustin Sainte-Beuve, the Goncourt Brothers and historian Joseph Ernest Renan on Chateaubriand steak and "champagne that was too expensive but so good that it was irresistible." It was over the rich food provided by the chefs at Bonfinger that Berlioz wrote his memoirs and composed his oratorio, *L'enfance de Christ*. In Italy, where he stayed in 1831 and 1832, he continued to write music at restaurants and cafés but did not take a liking to Italian restaurants, finding them "not up to the standards of Paris."

Berlioz' favorite dish was chicken fricassee, and if his diaries are to be believed, he sampled this dish in no less than three hundred and twenty Paris restaurants. The recipe that follows was dedicated to Berlioz by Casimir Moisson, the chief chef at the Café de Paris. The dish was served to Berlioz, Honoré de Balzac, the Goncourt Brothers and

several other friends on the night of October 12 1838, when they celebrated the Paris opening of Berlioz' opera, *Benvenuto Cellini*.

Suprêmes de Volaille Berlioz
Chicken Breasts Berlioz

FOR THE CHICKEN:

4 chicken breasts, halved along their seams

2 eggs, lightly beaten with 2 tsp water

¼ cup flour

¼ cup butter

1 cup chicken stock

1 cup sweet cream

juice of 1 small lemon

salt and pepper to taste

FOR THE ARTICHOKE HEARTS:

¾ lb (350 gr) mushrooms, chopped

2 Tbsp butter

2 Tbsp sweet cream

2 Tbsp onion, chopped

8 large or 16 small artichoke hearts, cooked, at room temperature

salt and black pepper to taste

Sprinkle the chicken with salt and pepper. Dip each half first in the beaten egg mixture and then in the flour to coat lightly.

In a skillet melt the butter and in this fry the breasts for about 5 minutes, turning once or twice. Add the stock and the sweet cream, bring just to a boil and reduce the flame to allow a low simmer for about 10 minutes. Remove from the heat and set aside to keep warm.

While the chicken is cooking prepare the artichoke hearts. In a skillet, melt the butter and in this sauté the onions and mushrooms until they have browned. Add the sweet cream and salt and pepper and heat through. With this mixture fill the artichoke hearts and place in a hot oven for 5 minutes.

To serve, place the chicken breasts on a warm serving plate, and pour over the sauce. Surround the chicken breasts with the artichoke hearts and serve piping hot. (Serves 4).

Les Œufs Berlioz
Eggs Berlioz

6 eggs, poached
6 slices of stale bread, each
 about 2½" (6 cm) thick
oil for frying
1 cup Madeira sauce (see p. 125)

3 Tbsp each truffles and
 champignon mushrooms,
 chopped coarsely
2 cups Duchess Potatoes (see
 p. 90)

First, make the croustades. Use a sharp knife to cut the bread slices into the shape of circular rolls. With a sharp knife cut a line around the roll near the top to mark what will become the lid of the croustade, and then fry the shaped rolls in deep oil until nicely browned. Remove with a slotted spoon, let drain on paper toweling and cool for a few minutes. With the sharp knife, gently cut off the lids and then spoon out and discard the interior of the baked roll, leaving a medium-thick shell intact. Scoop out and discard some of the crumbs from the lids.

In a saucepan combine the Madeira sauce, truffles and mushrooms and heat through. Add the Duchess Potatoes and stir gently, heating through and mixing well.

Fill the croustades with this mixture and then gently place a poached egg on top, followed by the lid of the croustade. Serve hot. (Serves 6 as a first course).

Soul Food

W hen I eat pork at a meal, give me the whole pig," wrote Nikolai Gogol, the nineteenth century Russian genius, in his masterpiece *Dead Souls*. On another occasion he commented that he had no use for "great gentlemen who live in the big cities and who spend their time in deliberating what fine foods they will eat tonight." Gogol preferred the healthy Slavic appetite to the delicate diets imported from the West, and indeed the characters in *Dead Souls* eat incessantly, their meals featuring all of Russia's traditional fare.

Chichikov, the protagonist of this grotesque tale, who spends long hours on the roads, "is wise enough to ask for ham at one post-station and suckling pig at another, and a portion of sturgeon or some smoked sausage and onion at a third. Later, when he finds an inn for the evening, as if he had eaten nothing at all for three days, he will request a stuffed chicken and, because a single chicken is never enough for one man, he will request as well a plate of cabbage, perhaps with a few sausages."

Chichikov eats heartily also at the tables of landowners, with whom he is negotiating ownership rights to their dead serfs. Sobakevitch, for example, gives him cabbage soup, sheep's stomach stuffed with

porridge and brains, and all sorts of entrées. That done, "the servants applied themselves to bringing in various comestibles under covers, through which could be heard the hissing of hot roast viands." When Chichikov lodges in the home of an old woman on a stormy night, he wakes to find the table "already spread with mushrooms, pies, fritters, cheesecakes, doughnuts, pancakes, open tarts with all sorts of different fillings, some with onions, some with poppy seeds, some with curds, and some with fish, and there is no knowing what else." Though these descriptions mock the gluttony of the landowners, reading them one cannot help but feel that Gogol rejoices in the ample nourishment of his beloved *Rus*.

Dostoyevsky once said, "We all came out from under Gogol's cloak" thus acknowledging his predecessor as the father of Russian literature. Gogol himself led quite an ascetic—one might even say miserable—life, haunted by poverty, real or imaginary rejection, and suffering from bouts of depression. In his last years Gogol resided in Rome, where he developed mystical and religious inclinations. Upon returning to Moscow in 1852 he destroyed the second volume of *Dead Souls*, refused to take any food and died in agony when he was only forty-two.

The following recipes, adapted from a nineteenth century Russian cookbook, would have pleased Chichikov.

Chicken Stuffed with Beef and Nuts

1 large chicken	2 Tbsp parsley, chopped
rind of 1 lemon, grated	5–6 oz. chopped almonds
1 large onion, chopped	½ cup oil
4 cloves garlic, chopped	2 tsp sweet paprika
1¼ lb (675 gr) chopped beef	salt and pepper to taste
6 Tbsp half-cooked rice	

Clean the chicken well, discarding the excess fat. Sprinkle lightly with salt, inside and out, and set aside for 1 hour. Rinse the chicken under cold water and dry well inside and out.

Combine the lemon rind, onion and garlic with the chopped beef. Add the rice, parsley, almonds and ½ tsp each of salt and pepper.

Mix well by hand. In a skillet heat ¼ cup of the oil and in this fry the mixture until the onions are translucent. Stuff the cavity of the chicken with the mixture and sew closed.

Place the stuffed bird in a baking dish and sprinkle generously with paprika and with salt and pepper to taste. With a brush, coat the chicken lightly with part of the remaining oil. Place the chicken in a hot oven, basting occasionally with the remaining oil and the pan drippings. The chicken will be reddish brown when ready (about 40 minutes). Serve hot. (Serves 4–6).

Sausages with Cabbage

2 lb (900 gr) lean, boneless
    pork
6 oz (175 gr) pork fat
About 2 tsp dried thyme
2 tsp finely ground black
    pepper
1 tsp salt

1 tsp dried basil
bacon fat for cooking
1 cup Béchamel sauce (see
    p. 67)
1 cup milk
4 cups cabbage, shredded finely

Grind the pork and the fat together. In a mixing bowl combine the pork and fat with the salt, pepper, thyme and basil. Blend together well. Shape the mixture into individual patties about 3″ (8 cm) in diameter and ½″ (1 cm) thick.

In a heavy skillet melt the bacon fat and in this fry the patties over a medium flame. Turn occasionally so that both sides cook evenly. Cook until the sausages are well browned on the outside and done inside. Drain off the excess fat as it accumulates, leaving about 1/8″ (¼ cm) of fat in the pan at any time. Drain the sausages on absorbent toweling. Set aside to keep warm.

Prepare the Béchamel sauce.

In a large saucepan bring the milk to a boil and into this gradually drop the cabbage. Boil for 2 minutes and then drain.

Discard the milk. Drop the cabbage into the hot Béchamel sauce, toss well and simmer for 2–3 minutes longer. Serve immediately by piling the sausages on top of the cabbage. (Serves 6).

Franz Sacher, 1816–1907

A Piece of Cake

Under the spell of the waltz and *Gemütlichkeit*, bakers in the cities along the Danube River created the richest and creamiest cakes and tortes, making Vienna and Budapest the undisputed capitals of the confectioner's art in nineteenth century Europe. The most famous, and perhaps the greatest Viennese pastry chef, was Franz Sacher, who used the money he made in his *konditorie* to construct the Hotel Sacher.

It was to this luxurious establishment, in one of Vienna's most prestigious neighborhoods, directly behind the Opera House—where it still stands today—that royalty and the wealthiest families of Europe made pilgrimages. Princess Anne of England wrote, "During the daylight hours we while away the time feasting on the marvelous cakes prepared by our host. At night we turn to the more serious business that takes place around the roulette wheel." Sacher, a fun-loving man who consumed enormous amounts of his own pastries and weighed well over 120 kilos, once wrote to a friend that he enjoyed "nothing more than light flirtations with the ladies, the incalculable joys of my bakery, an occasional love affair and, once in a while a visit to Paris, there to laugh at the inferior dining habits of our French cousins."

The only thing that would make Sacher angry would be if one

of his assistants failed to follow his instructions to the letter. At such moments, the usually jovial baker would fly into a rage and fling the nearest objects at hand at the offending employee. On one occasion this proved somewhat disastrous, as the cookie knife he threw at an assistant baker cut off the poor man's nose. Sacher avoided imprisonment only because he promised to pay a lifelong pension to his victim.

Whatever one thinks of his temper, the torte that carries Sacher's name is one of the most flavorful and rich cakes in the world. It was first created in 1832, when sixteen-year-old Sacher was working as an apprentice in the kitchens

of Austrian statesman Prince Klemens von Metternich. The prince asked for a speciel dessert cake for his dinner, and since the pastry chef was ill, young Franz did his best.

The Sachertorte became popular throughout Vienna and made Sacher a prosperous man. His son Eduard continued the tradition of serving the torte in the Hotel Sacher. In Vienna today the cake is made in countless cafés and bakeries but there are only two places that are permitted by law to write the name "Sacher" on the cake—the Café

Sacher in the Hotel Sacher and the Café Demel, where they serve a slightly different version. It is believed that Sacher, for one reason or another, sold the original recipe to the Demel family sometime in the nineteen century.

Sachertorte

FOR THE TORTE:

¾ cup butter, at room temperature
¾ cup sugar
½ lb (225 gr) semisweet chocolate, melted
8 egg yolks

10 egg whites at room temperature
¼ tsp salt
1 tsp vanilla extract
1¼ cups flour, sifted
¾ cup apricot preserves, pureed

FOR THE FONDANT ICING:

6 cups confectioners' sugar, sifted
½ cup water

2 Tbsp light corn syrup
1 tsp almond extract

In a mixing bowl cream the butter and then gradually add the sugar, beating until the mixture is light and fluffy. Add the chocolate and mix well. One by one beat in the egg yolks, mixing thoroughly with each addition.

Add the salt to the egg whites and beat until stiff. Fold the vanilla and ⅓ of the egg whites into the chocolate mixture.

Sift the flour again and fold into the batter alternately with the remaining egg whites. Pour the batter into a 10″ (25 cm) buttered spring form pan and bake in a medium oven until a toothpick inserted in the center comes out clean (35–45 minutes). Let cool in the pan for about 10 minutes.

Remove the ring and set the bottom of the pan on a cake rack. Let cool for several hours. When the cake is completely cool, spread with the apricot preserves and then cover the preserves with the fondant icing.

To prepare the icing, combine the sugar, water, corn syrup and almond extract. Cook over a high flame, skimming periodically, until the mixture has reached a temperature of 115 degrees Fahrenheit (45 degrees Celsius), using a cooking thermometer to check the temperature. Let the mixture cool for about 5–6 minutes and then pour it over the cake, turning the cake so that the icing coats it thoroughly. With a rubber spatula spread the icing over the sides of the cake. (Serves 6–8).

Charles Monselet, 1825–1888

Fooling the Critic

Like many restaurateurs, Paul Cohen-Brébant, who owned the popular Paris restaurant Brébant-Vachette, had a deep dislike for Charles Monselet, a well known journalist who often wrote biting, almost vindictive restaurant reviews. Many of Paris' true gourmets and chefs were sure that Monselet was merely a pretender and some went as far as to claim that he had no sense of taste at all.

In the spring of 1878, Cohen-Brébant decided to take his revenge, and invited Monselet to what was supposed to be a dinner in his honor. Chavette, the chef at the restaurant, prepared a special menu that included swallow's nest, brill, mountain goat cutlets and partridge. The wines listed on the hand-printed menu were a Clos Vougeot, a Tokai and a white wine from Africa's Cape of Good Hope. Cohen-Brébant shared his plan with three other famous guests, Edmond de Goncourt, Théophile Gautier and Joseph Hémard, who also detested Monselet.

Monselet raved over every dish and every wine. When the meal ended, as Hémard later wrote in a letter to a friend, the chef came to the table and loudly proclaimed that Monselet had made a complete fool of himself. The soup was nothing more than a puree of noodles and white beans; the brill was merely the cheapest cod that could be bought in the market; the mountain goat had been nothing more than lamb chops, and the partridge had been merely a small turkey. Even the wines that had Monselet in a nearly rhapsodic state had been fraudulent. The Clos Vougeot was an ordinary wine to which the chef had added a spoonful of cognac and a violet flower; the Tokai was a simple wine from Macon with some gin added, and the South African wine was cheap Chablis.

Several years later, Monselet was invited to an afternoon dinner party at the home of Joseph Favre, author of the *Grand Dictionnaire de Cuisine*, who was also a gifted cook. The menu consisted of liver of

burbot—a fresh water fish whose liver is especially prized by gourmets—Lyon sausages with Isigny butter; salmon escalopes with tartar sauce; and an omelet of ambergris—a grey, waxy substance found in the intestines of certain whales that is used in the making of fine perfumes.

Learning precious little from the earlier trick played on him, Monselet commended each dish until finally Favre confessed that the meal had been concocted from the carcass of a dead Egyptian crocodile he had been given the previous day while visiting the Paris zoo. The burbot livers were actually crocodile brains, the salmon escalopes, which Monselet had proclaimed with total self-assuredness were from Scotland, had been made from the tail of the crocodile, and the omelet had been made with its eggs. To increase Monselet's dismay, Favre also revealed that the Lyon sausages were made out of horsemeat, and that the Isigny butter was actually made with margarine.

Despite Monselet's obvious faults, many chefs dreaded his reviews and in order to flatter his ego and win his approval dedicated new dishes to him. One of the best known of these is the recipe for Bombe Monselet. Another is the omelet devised by French-born chef Dadou Mayer of Salsa del Salto in Taos, New Mexico.

Bombe Monselet

4 cups tangerine, mandarin or orange sorbet
1 cup candied orange peel, cut into small dice
½ cup Cognac, Armagnac or other high quality brandy

7 cups sugar
32 egg yolks
1 tsp vanilla extract
¼ cup Port wine
about 3 cups sweet cream, whipped stiff

Line a bombe mold or a ceramic bowl with the sorbet and place in the freezer until the sorbet is frozen solid.

In a small bowl soak the candied orange peel in the brandy.

In a saucepan dissolve the sugar in 4 cups of water. Bring to a rapid boil, strain and filter.

In the top of a large double boiler over but not in hot water combine the syrup and egg yolks, stirring regularly with a whisk. When the mixture becomes as thick as sweet cream rub it through a fine sieve into a clean bowl. Add the vanilla extract and then the Port and continue to stir until the mixture is cool. To this mixture add the candied peels and then an equal volume of the whipped cream. Place the mixture in a porcelain or ceramic container, cover and refrigerate until the mixture is completely cold (at least 4–5 hours). When cold fill the bombe mold with this mixture. Seal the mold and let stand in the freezer until solid throughout.

To serve, dip the mold into a large bowl of warm water for a few seconds and then turn onto a large, chilled serving plate. (Serves 12–16).

Œufs Monselet
Eggs Monselet

6–8 medium artichoke hearts, cooked until just tender, drained and quartered
4 Tbsp butter
3 Tbsp sweet cream
1 Tbsp each, fresh tarragon and dill, both chopped

4 eggs
1 Tbsp water
lemon and parsley for garnish
salt and pepper to taste
Béchamel sauce (see p. 67) for serving

In a large heavy skillet melt 2 Tbsp of the butter and in this sauté the artichokes until they take on a golden color. Remove from the flame, stir in the sweet cream and herbs, season to taste with salt and pepper, cover and set aside to keep warm.

In a mixing bowl, whisk together the eggs and water. In a clean skillet melt the remaining butter and when hot swirl the pan so that it coats the entire surface. Pour in the eggs and cook until the omelet has begun to set, pulling back the edges with a rubber spatula. Spoon over the artichoke mixture, fold the omelet and slide onto a serving plate. Spoon Béchamel sauce over the omelet, garnish with lemon wedges and parsley and serve at once. (Serves 2).

Empress Eugenie, 1826–1920

The Sweet Secrets
of the Boudoir

Described by her husband as the most marvelous of wives, a woman that "never complains, never raises her voice in anger, and never makes demands of any kind whatsoever," Eugenie, the wife of Napoleon III and Empress of France from 1853 until 1871, was viewed somewhat less favorably by one of her ladies-in-waiting. She wrote that the empress was "a woman so unconcerned with the pleasures or passions of life that it is difficult to know whether she is ill or merely stupid."

The truth was that Eugenie María de Montijo de Guzmán of Madrid simply did not care for her husband or the French people. In her memoirs, published a year before her death, she wrote: "My husband thought I was content. He was wrong. I only pretended to be comfortable in order to hide the fact that I loathed him." As to the French, she found them "dull compared to the Spanish and not nearly as charming as the Italians." She also detested "the soups and roasts and sauces and other such monotonies that so please the French" and although she would sit tolerantly through formal state dinners, she rarely ate anything in public. Like several other royal Europeans, Eugenie had a passion for

233

sweets, and after her guests had finished dining she would retire to her rooms, there to feast on six or more dessert dishes.

In 1874, a year after her husband died, Eugenie returned to Spain and her appetites returned. In addition to being a valued guest at dinner parties, she was frequently found at the fine restaurants of Madrid. Historian Juan Gayalo wrote that "even though she continued to be fond of sweets, the former empress now showered her devotions on large red lobsters served with butter and lemon, and omelets filled with crabmeat." For the rest of her life she avoided French food and French men and never again spoke the French language.

Riz a l'Imperatrice Eugenie
Rice à la Empress Eugenie

¼ cup glacéed fruits, chopped	pinch of salt
3 Tbsp kirsch liqueur	6 egg yolks
1 cup rice, well washed	½ cup sweet cream, whipped
7 cups milk	stiff
⅔ cup sugar	1 cup raspberry jam
¼ cup butter	1 cup vanilla custard
2 tsp vanilla extract	

In a small bowl, mix together the glacéed fruits and kirsch, stirring well. Let stand until ready for use (at least 1 hour).

In a large saucepan bring 2 quarts (4 liters) of water to the boil and in this boil the rice for 5 minutes. Drain, rinse under warm water and drain again.

In a flameproof casserole dish bring the milk, sugar, butter, vanilla and salt to the boil. To this add the rice and cook over a high flame for 5 minutes. Cover and transfer to an oven that has been preheated to low and cook until the rice is nearly tender. Remove from the oven, let cool for 20 minutes and then add the egg yolks, mixing in carefully with a fork. Taste and add sugar if necessary, and then let the rice cool. With the rice at room temperature, stir in the glacéed fruits and then fold in the vanilla custard. Gently fold in the whipped cream.

Lightly oil a ring mold and spread the bottom with a layer of raspberry jam about 1 centimeter deep. On top of this place the rice. Cover the mold with buttered wax paper and refrigerate overnight. When ready to serve, dip the mold into hot water for several seconds, taking care not to moisten the contents. Remove the wax paper and place a serving plate on the mold. Holding the mold tightly, quickly turn the plate over, thus turning the rice onto the plate. (Serves 4–6).

Variations: To make *Pêches a l'Imperatrice*, peel 8 peaches and poach them in vanilla flavored syrup for 5 minutes. Drain the peaches and arrange them around the rice. Refrigerate until well chilled and just before serving place a teaspoon of strawberry or raspberry jam on each. For *Abricots a l'Imperatrice* use poached, unpeeled apricots.

Frédéric Mistral, 1830–1914

Provincial Pleasures

P oet and Nobel Laureate Frédéric Mistral thrived on the physical beauty of his native Provence, but more than that, perhaps, on the beauty of the Provençal women. It was his habit, just before sunrise, to make his way to one of the cafés of Aix-en-Provence, Arles or Nimes with the woman he had bedded that night, there to wait for the proprietor to open his doors. After sharing a large breakfast, he would ceremoniously kiss her, shake hands, dismiss her with his best wishes for a good day, and then spend the rest of the day in the café drinking white wine and writing.

As he sat, he always kept a sharp eye on the women that came and went. If by nine in the evening Mistral had not arranged a rendezvous, he would stay on in the café until after the last waiter had wandered off home. This did not happen often, however. Fernand Rou, the owner of a small café in Arles wrote in a letter to his sister that "rarely have I known a man so successful with women. He would select his target; approach her openly with an invitation for several glasses of wine, a light dinner and an excursion to his bed. No matter how ladylike they might have been, the women seemed to find him impossible to resist."

Mistral's sexual potency astonished his friends, but so did his

conviction that drinking two bottles of white wine and eating a minimum of eight eggs daily would add to his vigor and longevity. Upon his death at the age of eighty-four, it was reported that during the previous week he had made love to four women and had eaten sixty-two eggs.

Mistral's love of eggs and of the cooking style of Provence inspired many local chefs to invent new dishes in his honor. The first recipe below was devised by the chef at Le Nègre-Coste, the oldest café-hotel in Aix, which still exists at 33 Cours Mirabeau. The second was dedicated to Mistral by a chef at the now closed Lou Marques restaurant in Arles.

Omelette Mistral

8 eggs
3 Tbsp mildly flavored olive oil
½ cup eggplant, peeled and
   diced
6 Tbsp butter

3 large tomatoes, peeled,
   seeded and diced
2 tsp parsley, chopped
1–2 cloves garlic, minced
salt and pepper to taste

In a skillet, heat the oil and in this sauté the eggplant until cooked through and soft. In a separate skillet heat 3 Tbsp of the butter and in this sauté the tomatoes until tender. Mix the eggplant and tomatoes together and add the parsley and garlic, mixing well.

In a mixing bowl lightly beat the eggs and season with salt and pepper. Add the tomato-eggplant mixture. In a large clean skillet melt the remaining butter and in this make a flat omelet in the usual manner. (Serves 4–6).

Œufs à la Mistral
Eggs à la Mistral

8 eggs
4 slices bread
2 Tbsp vegetable oil
½ cup butter

2 tsp each of fresh parsley, chives, tarragon and chervil, all chopped
salt and pepper to taste

From each slice of bread cut a 10 centimeter round. In a skillet heat the oil and 2 Tbsp of the butter and in this fry the bread until golden brown on both sides. Drain the fried bread on paper toweling, arrange on a serving platter and keep warm.

Whisk the eggs together with the salt and pepper until they are slightly frothy and then quickly beat in the herbs. In a heavy skillet melt the remaining butter and add the eggs, stirring constantly with a wooden spoon just until they begin to thicken. Stop stirring and cook just until the eggs are at the desired consistency. Spoon the eggs onto the fried bread rounds and serve immediately. (Serves 4–6).

Paul Marguery, 1832–1910

Merry Dining

I n 1877, Paul Marguery, until that point an unknown chef, bought a rundown café on Paris' Boulevard Bonne-Nouvelle. It took him nearly six months to rebuild and furnish the café, which he named after himself, and soon Marguery's had become the most popular place in Paris for banquets, political luncheons, reunions of old military comrades and bourgeois wedding feasts.

Meals at Marguery's were typified by a good deal of drinking, a great amount of noise and what one critic described as "an ever present but somewhat amusing vulgarity." Although some clients complained that the noise was distracting, and that the drunkenness displayed sometimes made it difficult to enjoy dinner, all were in agreement that the cuisine was superb. The restaurant also had what was probably the most extensive choice of wines in all of Paris, and, as an additional attraction, some of the waitresses were willing to pass an hour or two with male guests in the luxurious private rooms that were maintained on the second floor.

It is estimated that Marguery invented more than fifty dishes. The most popular and most often imitated of these was probably one known today as Sole Marguery, a dish described many years later by

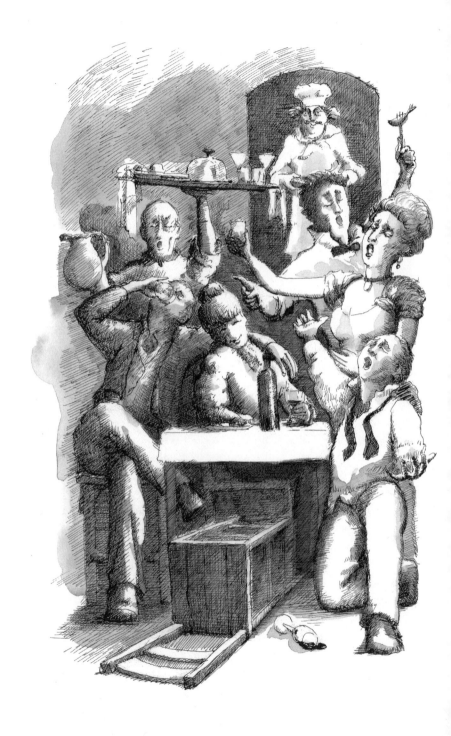

Georges Pompidou as "the epitome of French cuisine." Almost as well known is the sauce devised by Marguery and named for him.

Sole Marguery

4 large fillets of sole	¼ cup butter
12–16 mussels or clams, well scrubbed	3 Tbsp flour
12 large shrimps	½ cup sweet cream
2 cups dry white wine	2 egg yolks
4 shallots, chopped	salt and pepper to taste

In a small saucepan bring ¾ cup of water to a rapid boil. Plunge the mussels into the water, cover and steam until the shells open (about 5 minutes), discarding any of the mussels that remain closed. Remove the mussels from their shells. Strain and reserve the cooking liquids.

In a separate saucepan, plunge the shrimps into boiling water just until they turn pink (2–3 minutes), taking care not to overcook. Drain the shrimps, plunge under cold water, shell and de-vein them.

In a large skillet simmer the wine and shallots, covered, for 5 minutes. Place the sole fillets in the wine, season with salt and pepper, and simmer just until the fish is done, again taking care not to overcook. With a large spatula remove the fish gently to a preheated serving plate and set aside to keep warm. Strain and reserve the liquids.

In a clean saucepan melt 3 Tbsp of the butter and to this add the flour, stirring over a low flame for several minutes. Add about 1 cup of the wine in which the fish was cooked and stir until the mixture begins to thicken. Simmer very gently for 5 minutes and then add the mussels and shrimps. Remove from the flame.

In a small bowl beat together the egg yolks and cream and then slowly add some of the wine sauce to the bowl, mixing well. Place the pan with the sauce back on a very low flame, pour the egg and cream mixture into the sauce and stir until smooth and thick, taking care not to let the sauce boil. Remove from the flame and blend in the remaining butter. If the mixture is too thick, add a bit of the reserved liquids in which the mussels were cooked. Pour the sauce over the fish and serve immediately. (Serves 4).

Sauce Marguery

Considered ideal for spooning over fried or grilled fish fillets, grilled lobsters, coquilles St. Jacques, fried oysters or crab cakes.

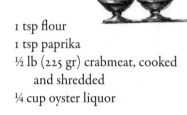

2 eggs yolks
1 cup butter, melted
juice of ½ large lemon
1 Tbsp water
20 small-medium shrimp,
    cooked, peeled and
    chopped
½ cup mushrooms, lightly
    sautéed in butter

1 tsp flour
1 tsp paprika
½ lb (225 gr) crabmeat, cooked
    and shredded
¼ cup oyster liquor

In a double boiler over hot but not boiling water beat the egg yolks with a wire whisk until fluffy. Add the melted butter very slowly, continuing to whisk until the mixture has thickened. Add the remaining ingredients, mixing well and heat through. Season to taste with salt and pepper and serve at once. (Yields about 1½ cups).

Alexander Etienne Choron, 1837–1924

Elephant Pie

Some French chefs are immortalized by the dishes that carry their names; others have streets or Metro stations named after them. In addition to more than twenty well-known dishes, two streets and two statues, Alexander Etienne Choron was also immortalized in art and literature; he was the model for the chef in Anatole France's *La Rôtisserie de la Reine Pédauque* as well as the baker who prepare cakes for Madame Bovary in Flaubert's novel, and is pictured in Manet's *Dejeuner sur l'Herbe*.

Acknowledged as one of France's greatest chefs, Choron ruled the kitchens at the Restaurant Voisin for many years. In this small restaurant on the corner of rue Saint-Honoré and rue Cambon he prepared dinners for a regular clientele that included Emile Zola, Gustave Flaubert, Charles Augustin Sainte-Beuve and Léon Daudet. As a confidant of the Goncourt brothers, two of the most celebrated literary figures of the time, Choron was frequently called in to plan and prepare the lavish lunches that the idiosyncratic brothers hosted for their friends.

The cellars of the restaurant were famous for their Burgundy and Bordeaux wines and the chef was renowned for his lamb dishes, roast beef, meat pies and baked chicken. Even during the siege of Paris in 1871, when food was extremely hard to come by for most Parisians, Choron made arrangement with an English butcher, Julius Roos, who supplied him with the finest meats and game that he could steal from the Paris Zoo. The Goncourt brothers frequently dined with their friend Arsène Houssaye on Choron's famous elephant pie.

When asked by a visiting Englishman for the recipe for this dish, Choron responded, "It is quite simple. All you need do is to roast the trunk or foot of an elephant in the same way you would roast a large piece of beef. When the meat is ready, dice it very finely and add a bit of boiling *demi-glace* sauce or other rich brown sauce. Heat the mixture in a *bain-marie* and, when it is cooked through, serve it in a pie dish." However, the regular patrons of the restaurant knew very well that Choron never roasted an elephant. His famous pies were actually made from the meat of pigeons he would trap on the roof of the building in which he resided.

The following dish, devised by Choron himself, takes a fairly long time to prepare, but the results are well worth the effort.

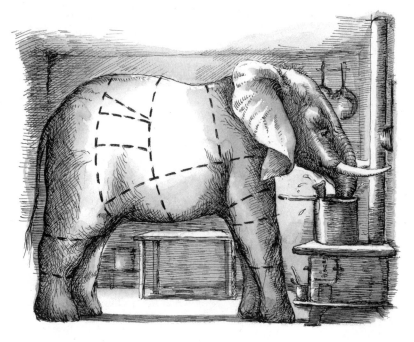

Tournedos Choron

4 tournedos or small fillet
    steaks
8 medium artichoke hearts
½ lemon
juice of 1 lemon
1 cup butter, at room
    temperature
½ lb (250 gr) peas

1 Tbsp melted butter
4 slices bread, without crusts
salt and pepper to taste
1 recipe for Choron sauce (see
    following recipe)
½ cup veal or chicken stock
3 Tbsp dry white wine

Rub the artichoke hearts with the lemon and cook them for 10 minutes in boiling salted water and half of the lemon juice. Drain. In a skillet melt 3 Tbsp of the butter. Add the artichoke hearts, cover the skillet and cook until the hearts are tender, turning once. (Cooking should take about 20 minutes).

Place the remaining lemon juice in a saucepan with about ½ centimeter of boiling water, add the peas and simmer, covered, just until the peas are tender, taking care not to overcook. Drain, and then sprinkle the peas with 1 Tbsp of melted butter. Shake the saucepan well, coating the peas.

In a skillet melt 2 more Tbsp of the butter and in this fry the bread slices, browning nicely on both sides, adding more butter only if the pan dries out.

Season the tournedos to taste with salt and pepper. In a heavy skillet melt 3 more Tbsp of the butter and in this sauté the tournedos over a high heat just until they are nicely browned on the exterior but still pink inside.

To serve: place the tournedos on the fried bread slices. Garnish with the artichoke hearts, filled with the peas. Pour a ring of Choron sauce around each tournedo. Add the stock and wine to the skillet in which the tournedos were cooked and heat through, scraping the bottom of the pan and stirring. Spoon about 1 Tbsp of this gravy over each tournedo and serve immediately. (Serves 4).

Sauce Choron

This sauce is ideal for steak, fish, chicken and egg-based dishes.

1½ cups Béarnaise sauce (see p. 49)

2–4 Tbsp tomato puree
Salt and pepper to taste

In a small bowl beat together the Béarnaise sauce and the tomato puree. Correct the seasoning with salt and pepper to taste. (Yields about 1½ cups).

Anna Deslions, 1838–1894

Anna à la Carte

I n all of France there is probably no courtesan more fondly recalled or respected than Anna Deslions who, in 1865, was deemed by the critic Sainte-Beuve to be "as true a queen as Paris has ever known." Deslions, who was known throughout Paris as *La Lionne des Boulevards*, was the model for the title character in Emile Zola's famous novel *Nana*.

Unlike her two major rivals, Valresse de la Bigne and Blanche d'Antigny, the beautiful and cultured Deslions never charged for her services, relying instead on the generous gifts that her clients bestowed upon her. This practice made good sense, because in addition to being generous with their cash, quite a few gave her diamond and emerald jewelry, several gave her sable coats, one gave her a cottage in Normandy, and another presented her with an apartment in London.

During Deslions' reign as "queen", the most fashionable restaurant in Paris was the Café des Anglais, an establishment favored by princes, emperors and society idols. Anna found the restaurant much to her taste, and the owner, Maurice Chevreuil, so adored her that he had a private dining room built for her on the second floor.

In addition to a table permanently set for two, the room also contained a large chaise longue and a comfortable canopied bed. Chevreuil,

who was a meticulous restaurateur, also kept a list of Deslions' lovers, including the crucial information as to what each of her lovers liked to eat and drink and at what time they had to be awakened to return home to their wives.

The still-famous dish known as *Pommes de Terre Anna* was named in her honor by Adolphe Dugléré, the most famous chef of the Café des Anglais. Dugléré also concocted several more dishes that he dedicated to Annette, a further homage to Anna who was known by this diminutive only to those with whom she had been intimate and a few close friends. It is said that three kings, twelve emperors, eighteen princes and thirty-four dukes knew the lady as Annette. According to the lists kept by Chevreuil, she was also known as Annette by two princesses and several well known actresses of the day.

Pommes de Terre Anna
Potatoes Anna

2 lb (900 gr) medium size potatoes, peeled and sliced as thinly as possible (but not soaked in water)

2 Tbsp vegetable oil
½ cup butter
salt and pepper to taste

In a shallow flame-proof casserole dish heat the oil and 2 Tbsp of the butter. Once the butter is melted, tip the casserole dish to coat the sides. Remove from the flame before the butter browns and arrange a single layer of potato slices in an overlapping spiral pattern.

Sprinkle over salt and pepper, and dot with butter. Continue building spiral layers. Salt and pepper each layer, and dot each with butter until the casserole dish is full.

Place the casserole dish over a medium flame and cook until the potatoes on the bottom layer are browned (about 12 minutes) and then transfer to a hot oven. While the potatoes cook, press them gently with a spatula from time to time, until they are tender when tested with a fork (about 25 minutes). To serve, loosen the edges with the spatula, place a preheated serving plate over the casserole dish and invert so that the potatoes fall on the platter. (Serves 6).

Omelette Annette

8 eggs
½ cup highest quality apricot
  or peach jam
1 tsp vanilla extract

salt and pepper as needed
4 Tbsp butter
6 Tbsp confectioners' sugar

In a saucepan heat the jam and keep it warm, ready for use.

In 4 separate small bowls, using a dinner fork, beat together 2 eggs, ¼ tsp of vanilla
extract and a pinch each of salt and pepper.
In a 9″ (23 cm) omelet pan (or similar heavy
skillet) melt 1 Tbsp of the butter and make
four omelets of 2 eggs each. (Add additional butter to the pan only if
it becomes dry). After each omelet is cooked, just before folding, spoon
in 2 Tbsp of the heated jam.

When the four omelets are done, place them on an oven-proof
serving plate, side by side. Sprinkle over the confectioners' sugar, place
in a hot oven just until the sugar begins to melt and serve at once.
(Serves 4).

Emile Zola, 1840–1902

One Good Meal Every Day

There is no image more romantic than that of the starving artist living in a garret in Paris, but the truth is that few artists ever actually came close to starvation. Still, Emile Zola was one who did. When he came to Paris in 1862 from Aix-en-Provence, he was so poor that he lived on nothing but bread and olive oil. For nearly three years, the only time he ate meat was when he was fortunate enough to trap one of the pigeons that landed on his windowsill.

With the publication of his first novel in 1873, his days of hunger ended, but his lean days had marked his work with a strong, sensual attitude towards food. *Le Ventre de Paris*, a novel that describes hopeless poverty, is set in the market of Les Halles. The book opens at dawn, as carts make their way to the market. Their drivers doze over the reins, leaning on huge piles of carrots and cauliflowers while their horses plod over familiar streets, until the contents of thousands of carts eventually work themselves into position and present voluptuous displays of fruits, fish, meats and cheeses. In *Nana*, Zola portrays an orgiastic party that his young heroine gives to celebrate her debut as an actress, making clear that the dinner, like Nana herself, is vulgar and decadent. Zola actually copied the menu for the meal, in which truffles were served with every

course, from
a press notice
of a dinner given
by Senator and
Madame de Freycinet
in 1878. His description
of the napkins, flowers
and footstools came from
real-life observation at Ber-
bant-Vachette, a restaurant then
highly popular with writers.

Zola himself gained a
reputation as a glutton once he
became rich and famous, epit-
omizing the most outrageous
aspects of the *Belle Epoque* he
professed to despise. He became
overweight, spent his time looking for exotic delicacies, and ate,
sometimes twice daily, at Paris'
best restaurants. In the company
of Daudet, Flaubert and de Maupassant, Zola dined frequently at
Magny, then the most famous
restaurant on the Left Bank,
and was also a regular
client at the exclusive
Maison Dorée on
the boulevard des

Italiens, where he would often start his dinner with a double portion of bouillabaisse before going on to a huge Chateaubriand steak. So dependent did Zola become on luxurious dining, that he was reduced to a state of misery if he could not look forward to at least one good meal every day. When he took refuge in England, after the Dreyfus affair, he wrote to Daudet: "No sauces, not enough salt, watery vegetables, poor spongy bread and bad puddings...I have been forced to take refuge in roast meat, ham, eggs and salads in order to survive."

It may be no more than mere coincidence but within two months of Zola's death both of his favorite restaurants, Magny and Maison Dorée, closed. The following dish was named after Zola by Georges Barthelemey, one of the sous-chefs at Magny.

Crème d'Asperges Emile Zola
Cream of Asparagus Soup Emile Zola

¾ lb (350 gr) asparagus,
   trimmed
½ cup butter
2 Tbsp flour
2½ cups chicken consommé

2 egg yolks
2 Tbsp sweet cream
pinch of sugar
salt and pepper to taste

Place the asparagus in a large saucepan and pour over enough water just to cover. Bring to a boil and then reduce the flame. Simmer just until the tips of the asparagus are tender. Drain, cut off the tender tips, and set aside.

Cut the stalks of the asparagus into ½" (1 cm) lengths. In a saucepan melt half the butter and in this cook the stalks, covered, until they are completely cooked. In a separate saucepan melt all but one 1 Tbsp of the remaining butter and into this stir the flour and then the chicken consommé. Bring to a boil, immediately reduce the flame and simmer gently for five minutes.

Pour about ½ cup of the stock mixture over the asparagus stalk and then liquidize the mixture in a food processor. Pour the liquidized asparagus through a strainer into the remaining stock. Reheat the mixture gently and season to taste with salt and pepper.

In a mixing bowl beat the egg yolks together with the cream and into these pour ½ cup of the hot soup, whipping vigorously with a wire whisk. Pour this mixture into the soup and heat over a moderate flame (without boiling) for 5 minutes. Add a pinch of sugar and correct the seasoning with salt and pepper to taste. Add the asparagus tips and heat through. Immediately before serving, float the remaining butter on the top of the soup.

The Prince of Wales, 1841–1910

Fair Game

A s a child, the Prince of Wales, Bertie to his friends, and later King Edward VII of England, was fond of horseback riding, cricket and quiet afternoon teas with his nannies. At the age of fifteen, however, he discovered that his true avocation was fornication, a sport to which he remained forever dedicated.

Being a member of the royal family, and the eldest son of Queen Victoria, his desire to couple with as many women as possible, as frequently as possible, was not always easy. During his time, men were obliged to confine sexual activities to women of the lower classes or to prostitutes, whose number in mid-nineteenth London boasted a quarter of a million. Bertie, who could not consort openly with such women, indulged instead in liaisons with married women, who were often invited to dine with him and his wife Alexandra. He is said to have had over hundred mistresses, the most famous of whom was the actress Lillie Langtry, who under his patronage became the brightest star on the London stage. Queen Alexandra's only criticism was to occasionally refer to him as "my naughty little man."

In addition to his insatiable sexual appetite, Bertie also had a passion for fine food. Considered something of a gourmet, he hired fine chefs for his kitchens and he would often travel to Paris, Baden-Baden and Venice to sample the fare of the famous restaurants of Europe, where chefs would vie to name dishes after him. When the great chef Escoffier took over the kitchens at the London's Savoy Hotel, the Prince of Wales dined there frequently, sometimes as often as five times weekly. It is said that one of his favorite dishes was Escoffier's *Nymphes a l'Aurore*, a dish that had little to do with nymphs, it being frogs' legs in Champagne jelly.

However, when it came to food, Bertie did have two odd habits. He invariably had a platter of sandwiches placed at his bedside before he retired so he could ease his hunger upon waking up in the middle of the night, and he was one of very few people who believed in decanting Champagne. The prince also had a special passion for coffee, and once, commenting on the differences between France and Germany he said: "You can tell when you have crossed the frontier into Germany because of the badness of the coffee."

When Edward was finally crowned in 1901, at the age of sixty, he was so overweight that it was impossible for him to button the lowest button of his jacket. His subjects, who adored him, left their lowest buttons undone as well, in homage.

The credit for the soup that follows, now a world-famous dish, was claimed by no fewer than eight chefs and two of Edward's mistresses. The origin of the fish dish is easier to trace, having been created in 1914 by chef Victor Herzler of San Francisco's St. Francis Hotel.

Consommé Edward VII

Note: Because two parts of this dish have to be cooked a full day before serving, please read the entire recipe before starting the preparation.

FOR THE MUSHROOM ROYALE:
½ Tbsp butter
4–6 large mushroom caps, chopped finely

2 tsp Béchamel sauce (see p. 67)
3 Tbsp sweet cream
4 egg yolks

FOR THE CHICKEN LOAF:
1 lb (450 gr) chicken meat, boned
1½ tsp salt

½ tsp white pepper
2 egg whites
3¼ cups sweet cream

FOR THE CONSOMMÉ:
8 cups chicken consommé
¼ cup tapioca

2 Tbsp Port wine

Prepare the Mushroom Royale: (To be prepared 24 hours before serving). In a small skillet, heat the butter and in this sauté the mushrooms for 2–3 minutes. Over a very low flame, stirring constantly, add the Béchamel sauce and sweet cream. Put the mixture through a sieve, add the egg yolks, and pour into a small mold that has been buttered in advance. Place the mold in the top part of a double boiler and cook over hot water just until the mixture is firm. Let cool and refrigerate overnight. Just before using, unmold and cut into small dice.

Prepare the chicken loaf: (To be prepared 24 hours before serving). Season the chicken with salt and pepper, chop coarsely and pound finely in a mortar. While pounding, slowly add the egg whites. Rub the mixture through a fine sieve and then stir vigorously with a wood spoon. Refrigerate for 2 hours.

Place the chicken mixture in a small bowl and place this in a larger bowl that has been filled with ice. Add the cream, a little at a time, stirring well. When all the cream has been added pour the mixture into a buttered ring mold, filling to about ½" of the top.

Fill an oven pan with about 1" (2½ cm) of water and place the ring mold in the water. Place in a low oven and cook until the mixture is set (about 1 hour). Remove from the oven, let stand 15–20 minutes and turn out. Cover lightly and refrigerate overnight.

Prepare the consommé: In a saucepan bring the consommé to the boil and then, stirring well, sprinkle in the tapioca. Boil gently for 18 minutes and then strain through muslin or a fine sieve. To serve, stir in the Port and then garnish the consommé with thin slices of the chicken loaf and the Mushroom Royale. (Serves 8).

Sole Edward VII

4 fillets of sole
½ lb (225 gr) butter, softened
¼ lb (115 gr) mushrooms,
    chopped
3 oz (85 gr) salted almonds,
    chopped

2 Tbsp parsley, chopped
juice of 1 large lemon
¼ cup dry white wine
salt, pepper and grated nutmeg
    to taste

Butter a large baking pan and on this lay the sole fillets.

In a bowl mix together the butter, mushrooms, almonds, parsley, lemon juice and salt, pepper and nutmeg to taste. Divide this mixture and spread over the fillets. Sprinkle over the white wine and place in an oven that has been pre-heated to medium-hot until the fish is done (about 20 minutes). Transfer the fillets and their topping to a serving platter that has been covered with a cloth napkin, spoon over some of the sauce and serve at once. (Serves 4).

Georges Auguste Escoffier, 1846–1935

Turning the Tables

A chef who had more impact on modern cuisine than any other, a culinary innovator of the first order, a brilliant restaurateur as well as inveterate impresario, and probably the first celebrity chef, Georges Auguste Escoffier once summed up his approach to gastronomy by saying that it "defines man as a superior species because he is the only animal who cooks his food and because he is capable of eating when he is not hungry."

Born to a family of blacksmiths in the village of Villeneuve-Loubet in Provence, at the age of thirteen he went to work in his uncle's restaurant in the nearby city of Nice. At nineteen he moved to Paris, where he quickly became a well-known sauce chef at the smart restaurant Le Petit Moulin Rouge. By 1880, at the age of thirty-four, he had become the best known chef in Europe. Royalty and socialists flocked to dine in his restaurants, Le Faisan d'Or in Cannes, at the Grand Hotel at Monte Carlo, and at the Hotel National in Lucerne, where he first met gifted hotelier César Ritz. Their partnership, one that would last twenty years, was well timed; the wealthy were craving new tastes, and Ritz and Escoffier were remarkably attuned to satisfy them.

In 1890 the pair took over the Savoy Hotel in London, and it instantly became the most highly esteemed hotel in Europe. In 1898 they opened the Ritz Hotel in Paris, and a year later the Carlton in London, where Escoffier had a team of sixty cooks serving up to five hundred diners at each meal. At the Carlton, where he would stay for twenty years, Escoffier became the first to introduce the à la carte menu. Further ventures included the Grand National Hotel in Rome as well as the Ritz hotels in London, New York, Philadelphia, Montreal and Johannesburg. Escoffier also spent some time in charge of the galleys of the Hamburg-Amerika luxury liner, the Imperator, where he was known to have produced a superb dish of salmon steamed in champagne for Kaiser Wilhelm II. "How can I repay you?" asked the emperor. "By returning Alsace-Lorraine to France" was Escoffier's reply. The Kaiser, instead, gave him the ultimate compliment: "I am the Emperor of Germany, but you are the Emperor of Chefs."

Escoffier is credited with inventing hundreds of dishes, but more than that, he is remembered as the man who revolutionized French cuisine. He modernized the overly elaborate and ornate haute cuisine dishes of the eighteenth century chef Marie-Antoine Carême, simplifying the complicated sauces, emphasizing the use of seasonal ingredients and developing the *brigade de cuisine*, the system that divides the kitchen into separate sections, each section run by a different sous-chef. He also replaced the *service à la Française* (serving all dishes at once) with *service à la Russe* (serving each dish in the order printed on the menu). These are the usual standards by which fine restaurant kitchens are organized to this day. His *Guide Culinaire,* a compendium of about five thousand recipes which was published in 1903, is considered the bible of all serious chefs to this day.

One of Escoffier's most famous dishes is Peach Melba, which was named in honor of Australian soprano Nellie Melba. After attending her performance of Wagner's *Lohengrin* in 1894, Escoffier designed a dessert of peaches and vanilla ice cream featuring a magnificent ice swan, to echo the swan featured in the opera, and named it *Pêche au Cygne* (peach with swan). A few years later, with the opening of the Carlton hotel, he eliminated the swan, topped the peaches with raspberry sauce and re-named it *Pêche Melba*. Another of his well-known dishes, Cherries Jubilee, was once dated to Queen Victoria's visit to the

French Riviera in 1882, during which she dined at the Grand Hotel in Monte Carlo. Some claimed, however, that Escoffier first introduced the dish for the queen's Golden Jubilee in 1887, and indeed, that date was confirmed by Escoffier himself.

Pêches Melba
Peach Melba

6 large fresh peaches, halved and peeled
3½ cups sugar
1½ tsp vanilla extract

1 lb (450 gr) raspberries, pureed
½ cup currant jelly
4 cups finest quality vanilla ice cream

Prepare a sugar syrup by adding the sugar to 2 cups of water and bringing to a rolling boil. Add the vanilla extract, let cool for several minutes, strain and filter. Into this place the peach halves and let stand until the syrup is cool. Refrigerate until well chilled.

In a small saucepan gently heat the raspberries and currant jelly together just until the jelly has melted. Let cool to room temperature.

Line individual dessert bowls or silver plates with a thick layer of vanilla ice cream. Remove the peach halves from the syrup with a slotted spoon, and let drain. In the center of the ice cream lay a peach half, cut side facing down, and generously spoon over the raspberry sauce. Ideally served with sweetened whipped cream. (Serves 6).

Cherries Jubilee

1 cup preserved cherries, pitted
¼ cup highest quality Cognac
2 Tbsp kirsch liqueur

1 pint (½ liter) highest quality vanilla ice cream

In an attractive skillet heat the cherries. While the cherries are heating, preheat the Cognac in a small saucepan. When the cherries are quite well heated, pour over the warmed brandy and carefully flame. Allow the flames to burn out and then add and stir in the kirsch. Serve by spooning the cherries in their sauce over individual portions of vanilla ice cream. (Serves 4–6).

Strawberries Americaine

During his tenure at the Carlton Hotel in London, Escoffier made an adaptation to Carême's *Fraises Romanoff* by adding vanilla ice cream to the dish. Afterwards, however, Escoffier's version was re-named quite a few times by various chefs in the United States, each of whom claimed credit for the dessert. The American version probably originated at Romanoff's restaurant in Beverly Hills, California, where the owner, the self-entitled Prince Michael Romanoff (who had no connection with the Romanoff family), "borrowed" the recipe and claimed it as his own. A chef at the Los Angeles Biltmore Hotel re-named it "Strawberries Biltmore", and another chef, in San Francisco's Palace Hotel, altered it completely by serving the dish with anisette and maraschino. Despite those changes, this altered dish also still carries the name "Strawberries Americaine."

2 pints strawberries, washed, hulled and halved (if very large, sliced)
¼ cup sugar

¼ cup Grand Marnier liqueur
2 pints vanilla ice cream
1 cup whipping cream

In a mixing bowl gently toss three-quarters of the strawberries with the sugar and liqueur. Refrigerate for 1–2 hours. Let the remaining strawberries stand at room temperature. During this time transfer the ice cream from the freezer to the refrigerator to soften.

Transfer the sweet cream and half of the chilled strawberries into a pre-chilled mixing bowl. With an electric mixer whip the mixture until soft peaks are formed and then fold in the ice cream. Distribute this mixture into 6 or 8 chilled dessert bowls. Mix those berries that were left to stand at room temperature with the remainder of those that were chilled and place these on top of the cream. Serve at once. (Serves 6–8).

Guy de Maupassant, 1850–1893
In the Flesh

No author has better championed the merits of fine dining than Guy de Maupassant. In one of his short stories, "Madame Husson's Rosier", Maupassant summed up his feelings when he wrote: "the sense of taste, my friend, is very delicate, capable of perfection, and quite as worthy of respect as the eye and the ear. A person who lacks this sense is deprived of an exquisite faculty, the faculty of discerning the quality of food, just as one may lack the faculty of discerning the beauties of a book or of a work of art...a man who cannot distinguish one kind of lobster from another, a herring...from a mackerel or a whiting, and a Cresane from a Duchess pear, may be compared to a man who mistakes Balzac for Eugene Sue and a symphony of Beethoven for a military march..."

Maupassant was a very prolific writer, and his short stories made him a wealthy man. He could afford to dine at the finest restaurants of Paris but was devoted exclusively to Magny, the smart restaurant on Paris' rue Mazet. Only when Charles Drouant opened his eponymously-named restaurant in 1880, did he began to divide his evenings between the two places. He also often lunched on the second level of the then new Eiffel tower, not so much because he liked the food but because, as did many of the Frenchmen of his time, he had a passionate dislike for the edifice and ironically, it was the only place in Paris where he did not have to see "this damned tower."

It is said that only on one occasion did Maupassant deviate from his regular dining habits. That happened when he had nearly completed

writing a short story about a murderer who decides to destroy the evidence against him by eating the corpse of the victim. If the story is to be believed, the author bribed an attendant at the Paris morgue, brought a human arm back to his apartment, cooked it, ate it and only then finished writing the story.

Maupassant contracted syphilis during his mid-twenties but that did not interfere with his lust for life. Rich and famous, he felt that he had become entitled to nearly all that he wanted. In 1889, dining at a restaurant with Henry James in London he saw a beautiful woman seated at a nearby table, pointed at her and in anything but subdued tones asked his host to "get her" for him. The syphilis did eventually take its toll, and six months before his death at the age of forty-three Maupassant tried to commit suicide and was committed to a private asylum where he died.

Magny closed his restaurant in the year of Maupassant's death, but Drouant, located at place Gaillon in the 2nd Arrondisement, remains a well known Paris establishment to this day. The restaurant still features such dishes as quail with blueberries, lobster mousse, and calf's liver with mushrooms, all among Maupassant's favorites.

Mousse Froid d'Homard
Cold Lobster Mousse

1 lobster, about 1½ lb (675 gr)	½ cup sweet cream
3 oz (85 gr) of scallops	½ tsp chives, snipped
(coquilles Saint Jacques)	½ tsp lobster roe (optional)
½ tsp sea salt	

Plunge the lobster into a kettle of boiling water and cook it, covered, for 1 minute. Transfer the lobster with tongs to a large bowl of ice and cold water, let it cool and drain it well. Break off the claws, crack them and remove the meat from the claws and the tail and in a food processor puree the meat together with the scallops and salt, scraping down the sides. With the motor running add the sweet cream in a stream and blend the mixture for 5 seconds. (Do not over-process or the mixture will separate). Force the mousse through a fine sieve into a bowl and then stir in the chives and lobster roe. Cover and chill the mousse for at least 1 hour and up to 8 hours before using. (Serves 4 as a first course).

Foie de Veau aux Champignons
Calf's Liver with Mushrooms

1½ lb (675 gr) calf's liver, sliced
    thinly
About ½ cup flour
2 Tbsp butter
1 Tbsp olive oil
½ lb (225 gr) Chanterelle
    or forest mushrooms,
    chopped finely
1 Tbsp parsley, chopped finely
1 Tbsp chives, snipped

1 clove garlic, crushed
1 Tbsp lemon juice
salt and pepper to taste

Place the flour on a plate and season it generously with salt and pepper. One at a time dip the liver slices in the flour and coat them well.

    In a large skillet heat the butter and oil and in this mixture fry the liver slices for about 3 minutes on each side (keep in mind that the liver should be pink inside after it is cooked). Transfer the liver to a preheated serving plate, cover and set aside to keep warm.

    Reheat the butter and oil mixture (if the skillet has dried out add 1 Tbsp more of butter) and then add the mushrooms, parsley, chives, garlic and lemon juice and continue to cook for 5 minutes longer, stirring often. Spoon the mushroom mixture over the liver and serve immediately, ideally with a dry red wine. (Serves 4).

William O'Brien, 1852–1928

The Perfect Irishman

T here could be no better prototype for the ideal Irishman than William O'Brien, a journalist who was a major figure in the Irish nationalist movement in the late nineteenth century. He represented different Irish constituencies in the British Parliament for more than thirty years, was arrested several times for political offenses, and spent over two years in prison but, as he wrote in his diary, "no one required me to serve in the role of a martyr."

As a young man, O'Brien wrote for the *Cork Daily Herald* and later for *Freeman's Journal*, and was described by James Reade, one of his editors, as "never accurate enough in his reporting to win a prize but never inaccurate enough for me to fire him." After meeting Charles Parnell, the president of the Irish Land League, in 1881, O'Brien became the editor of the League's militant journal, *United Ireland*.

The kind of journalist who would have belonged comfortably in a Damon Runyon novel, O'Brien frequently came to his office at the newspaper with one or two of his lady friends on his arm. He always carried a bottle of whiskey in his jacket pocket and was rarely known to be completely sober. One colleague wrote that "he was as charming as any Irishman could be—his tweed jacket was rarely pressed, his shirts

never clean and his shoes never polished, but he always had a good word for the janitor and the men who worked on the printing press."

During the rare times that he was "in the money", O'Brien enjoyed going by train to Hunter's Hotel in County Wicklow, there to drink Irish whiskey and to feast on freshly caught trout and strawberry pie. When friends were willing to foot the bill, he frequented the even more expensive Great Southern Hotel in County Kerry, where he always ordered the same dinner. He would start with a small trout, go on to vegetable soup and then to a generous portion of lamb that was served with broccoli, cauliflower and potatoes. To finish his meal he would have an orange mousse, coffee and half a bottle of whiskey. When he was low on cash, as was often the case, he took his meals in neighborhood pubs, enjoying in such places the traditional dish known the world over as Irish stew.

No one knows whether the dish that carries his name was created in his honor, perhaps by a hotel chef or a cook at one of the pubs he frequented. Some believe that the dish was devised in honor of another O'Brien, William Smith O'Brien, who led the Irish revolt of 1848. Others claim that the dish originated in New York at the beginning of the twentieth century. In any case, the dish has become an Irish standard, and in addition to being served in nearly every pub in the country it is also offered at both of the hotels O'Brien enjoyed visiting. The second dish was devised by New Orleans chef Paul Prudhomme.

Potatoes O'Brien

4 large potatoes, unpeeled but
    well washed
2 sweet red peppers

½ cup + 2 Tbsp butter
salt and pepper to taste

Place the red peppers over an open flame or under a hot grill and, turning several times, let the skin blacken. Remove, run under cold water and peel off the skin. Halve the peppers, discard the seeds and pith and then cut the peppers into small dice. In a small skillet heat 2 Tbsp of the butter and in this sauté the peppers for 2–3 minutes. Remove from the flame.

Place the potatoes in a pot with a large amount of lightly salted, rapidly boiling water. Let the potatoes boil just until tender. Drain, cool, peel the potatoes and cut them into dice. In a large heavy skillet melt the butter and in this sauté the potatoes until they are nicely browned. Season to taste with salt and pepper, add the red peppers and heat through, stirring regularly. Serve hot. (Serves 4–6).

Omelet O'Brien

6 eggs
6 Tbsp butter
3 cups O'Brien potatoes (see
    recipe on previous page)
½ tsp celery salt
¼ cup milk

½ tsp salt
½ cup Cheddar cheese, grated
¼ cup green onions, chopped
    coarsely
4–6 slices bacon, fried crisp
    and then broken into bits

In a large skillet melt 3 Tbsp of the butter. Add the potatoes and sprinkle with celery salt. Over a medium flame, stir gently but regularly until the potatoes are heated through.

    In a bowl lightly beat the eggs, milk, salt and pepper together. In a clean skillet melt the remaining butter. When the butter begins to sizzle pour in the egg mixture and cook over a medium heat. As the eggs begin to set, lift the edges, letting the uncooked portion flow underneath. When the eggs are cooked almost to the desired point distribute the potato mixture on the surface. Sprinkle over the cheddar cheese, green onions and bacon bits, cut into wedges and serve at once. (Serves 4).

Beyond Madeleines

E ven those that have not read Marcel Proust's monumental
work *À la Recherche de Temps Perdu* know the story of how the crumbs
of a Madeleine cookie in a teaspoon triggered in him "the vast struc-
ture of recollection" that gave birth to one of the world's great literary
works. "And suddenly the memory revealed itself," he writes, "the taste
was that of the little piece of Madeleine which on Sunday mornings at
Combray...when I went to say good morning to her in her bedroom, my
aunt Léonie used to give me, dipping it first in her own cup of tea or
tisane...and the whole of Combray and its surroundings, taking shape
and solidity, sprang into being...."

Oddly enough, as an adult, Proust was fond of neither tea nor
cookies. Even as a child, he never really enjoyed the "dainty, small things
that seem perfectly in place on delicate lace tablecloths." His tastes were
far more robust. Well known for his hearty appetite, Proust had a special fondness for the regional cooking of the Loire valley, a cuisine that
for at least three hundred years has relied heavily on wild game, the
fish of the Loire River, fresh fruits and the generous use of fresh herbs.
Among his favorite dishes were roast wild duck with fresh pineapple,

venison with mandarin oranges, and oysters prepared in almost any conceivable way.

On one occasion when traveling with friends, he stopped at a small restaurant in Orleans, where he dined on oysters with wild mushrooms, guinea hen with peaches, and rabbit in red wine sauce. During the pleasantly warm months of spring and summer, he especially enjoyed dining out-of-doors at restaurants with a view of the river. When he was vacationing, Proust especially enjoyed visiting the towns of Remorantin and Bracieux, both of which had comfortable inns and excellent restaurants.

The luxurious chateaux and extensive fruit orchards of the Loire Valley continue to attract people today, and like the gentle pace of life there, the cuisine of the region has also remained constant over the years. Both Remorantin and Bracieux have maintained their good culinary name, and one can still dine on many of the dishes that Proust so enjoyed. Among the dishes mentioned by the author as his favorites are goose breast with clementines, rabbit terrine, roast shrimps with chives and cinnamon butter, and spiced fresh codfish.

Crevettes au Beurre de Ciboulette et Cannelle
Shrimps with Chive and Cinnamon Butter

FOR THE SHRIMP:

16 very large or 24 medium shrimps, peeled
1 cup sweet cream
4 green cabbage leaves
4 small potatoes, peeled, sliced thinly and soaked overnight in cold water
½ cup clarified butter
2 Tbsp butter, at room temperature
2 cups vegetable oil for deep frying
1 cup flour
4 radishes sliced thinly and sprinkled over with safflower or other oil

FOR THE CHIVE AND CINNAMON BUTTER:

Pinch of salt
½ teaspoon ground cinnamon
½ cup butter, cut into pieces
2 Tbsp fresh chives, finely chopped

Prepare the shrimp: Place the shrimp and sweet cream in a mixing bowl and set aside. In a saucepan bring 3 cups of salted water to a rapid boil and into this plunge the cabbage leaves for 2–3 minutes. Remove the leaves and place in a bowl of ice water to cool. Drain and set aside.

Drain and dry the potato slices and brush them generously with the clarified butter. Arrange the potatoes in a single layer on a baking pan and bake in a medium-hot oven until they are crisp and golden (15–20 minutes). Remove from the oven and keep warm.

Prepare the chive and cinnamon butter: To a small saucepan containing 2 Tbsp of cold water add the salt and cinnamon and heat over a low flame. Add the butter, a few pieces at a time, beating constantly with a whisk. After all of the butter has been added, add the chives. Remove from the flame and keep warm.

In a heavy skillet heat the oil. One at a time remove the shrimp from the cream and coat them lightly with flour. Deep fry the shrimp in the hot oil for 1–2 minutes. Remove the shrimp with a slotted spoon. (If the shrimps are very large cut them in half). In a heavy saucepan heat 2 Tbsp of butter and in this cook the cabbage leaves until they are soft (3–5 minutes), taking care not to let them brown.

To serve: Fold the cabbage leaves and place them in the center of 4 warm plates. Arrange the potato slices on top of the cabbage and surround with the shrimps. Decorate the plates with the radish slivers and spoon over the chive and cinnamon butter. (Serves 4).

Terrine de Lapin
Rabbit Terrine

1 large rabbit, about 4½–5½ lb (2–2½ kilos)
½ lb (225 gr) lean pork, cut into chunks
½ lb (225 gr) bacon, cut into ½" (1 cm) cubes
6 thin slices bacon

1 large onion, peeled and quartered
2 Tbsp parsley, chopped
2 tsp thyme, chopped
6 juniper berries, crushed
2 cloves garlic, crushed
salt and black pepper to taste
¼ cup dry red wine
2 Tbsp brandy or Cognac

Bone the rabbit and cut the meat from the back into strips. Set the meat from the back aside. Remove the remaining meat from the bones and in a food processor mince this together with the pork, bacon cubes and onion. Combine the minced ingredients with the parsley, thyme, juniper, garlic, salt and pepper to taste, wine and brandy and mix well. Grease a 1.5 liter terrine dish well. Place half the mince mixture in the base of the terrine, pressing it down evenly. Lay the reserved strips of meat and the sliced bacon on top and then spoon the remaining minced mixture into the terrine. Smooth this pâté down evenly and then cover with a piece of greased aluminum foil and put the lid on the terrine.

Pour hot water into a large rectangular oven dish to a depth of 1" (2½ cm). Stand the terrine in the oven dish and bake in an oven that has been preheated to low for 2½ hours. Remove from the oven and place weights evenly on top of the aluminum foil. Let cool and then refrigerate overnight. Remove the weights and put the lid back on the terrine. Store in the refrigerator until required. (Serves 10–12).

Curnonsky, 1872–1956

The Prince

Lf anyone came to represent the gay ostentation of the boulevards of Paris and the passions of *La Belle Époque* it was Maurice Edmond Sailland, one of France's great gastronomes, known by his pen name Curnonsky. In 1890, when he was eighteen, he left his home in Angers and came to Paris to study at the *Ecole Normale Superieure* but spent most of his time in newspaper offices and in literary circles, making friends wherever he went. Soon enough he started to write and by 1914 was writing for several newspapers on various subjects, including food. He quickly became the most popular and respected culinary writer in all of France.

Co-authoring, with Marcel Rouff, the twenty-eight volume *France Gastronomique*, a guide to French regional cookery, gave him the opportunity and platform to state many of his rules of cooking, still followed today by many chefs. One of his best known statements was that "a classical meal should begin with creatures of the sea, progress to creatures of the sky, to creatures of the field and then to the mountains," by mountains referring to game meats such as deer and wild boar. It was there as well that he gave advice to travelers: "Whenever you get to a town and want to know the best place to eat, consult the local doctor and especially the priest. They know the best places."

In 1927 a public referendum crowned Curnonsky "Prince of Gastronomes" and from that moment he became a household name throughout France. Fifty culinary academies and clubs vied for his presidency and solicited his presence at their banquets. Cur, as he was known to his friends, indulged in this fame. His white napkin knotted bib-like under his collection of chins, he became a familiar figure in every restaurant of Paris.

Gertrude Stein wrote that he resembled a "physically amorphous creature, not dissimilar to an unfinished tub of butter."

Curnonsky was known for his pomposity and liked to issue forth proclamations such as "never eat the left leg of a partridge, for that is the leg it sits on, which makes the circulation sluggish." He was also known to walk into a restaurant and order a leg of lamb, insisting that the meat should be "as pink as a baby's backside."

When asked by a Paris hostess how he liked his truffles, Curnonsky replied, "in great quantity, Madame, in great quantity."

As a critic, Curnonsky was so feared that some restaurateurs considered a negative review from him reason enough to close their doors permanently. At the height of his career no less than eighty French restaurants held a table free every night just in case he showed up. He himself always stayed true to his principles. Upon being offered an enormous lifetime income simply for stating that margarine was as good as butter, he ceremoniously tore the check in half, stating that "nothing can ever replace butter."

Curnonsky wrote more than sixty-five books about cooking, as well as numerous articles. In 1930 he founded and became the first President of the *Académie des Gastronomes*, and in 1946 he began the magazine *Cuisine et Vins de France* in which he attempted to identify and promote the principles of fine dining. It was in that magazine that he delineated the hierarchy of French cuisine—haute cuisine, *la cuisine bourgeoise, la cuisine régionale*, and *la cuisine improvisée*, and suggested that in cooking, as in the arts, simplicity is a sign of perfection, and good cuisine means that "things have the taste of what they are."

In his later years he was so heavy that six friends had to carry him to his favorite restaurants. When, at the age of eighty-four, he fell from the balcony of his Paris apartment to his death, some speculated that the great gourmet had committed suicide because he could no longer taste or digest the food he so loved.

Most of the dishes dedicated to him are adaptations of well-known regional dishes. Several restaurants in Bordeaux continue to feature one of Curnonsky's favorites, a dish of sautéed rabbit with mustard sauce, and Le Chapon Fin still serves *livre à la royale Curnonsky*, a dish based on wild hare that takes seventy-two hours to prepare.

Gigot d'Agneau à la Curnonsky
Leg of Lamb à la Curnonsky

1 leg of lamb, about 5½ lb (2½ kilos)
1 clove garlic, halved
2 Tbsp vegetable oil
1 medium onion, quartered
1 large carrot, quartered
salt and pepper to taste

1 cup fresh breadcrumbs
4 Tbsp parsley, chopped
1 clove garlic, chopped finely
6 Tbsp butter, melted
6 Tbsp white wine
1½ cups beef stock

Trim the skin and all but a thin layer of the fat from the lamb and rub the leg well with the halved garlic clove. Into a large roasting pan place the oil, onion and carrot, and on these place the lamb. Sprinkle well with salt and pepper and roast in a very hot oven just until browned (10–15 minutes). Reduce the oven temperature to hot and continue roasting, basting frequently, adding a bit of stock if the pan dries out. Allow a total of 30–35 minutes per kilo for medium-rare meat.

Remove the lamb from the oven 10 minutes before the end of cooking and set the meat on a platter. Mix together the breadcrumbs, parsley and chopped garlic and spread evenly over the meat. Sprinkle with the melted butter and then return to the pan. Return to the oven for 10 minutes longer, or until the coating is lightly browned.

Transfer the lamb to a serving platter and let stand at room temperature for 10 minutes before carving.

While the meat is standing, make the gravy. First drain off the excess fat from the pan and discard the carrot and onion. Add the wine and 1 cup of stock. Bring to the boil, stirring well to dissolve the pan juices, and then simmer gently for 5–10 minutes, stirring occasionally. Strain and again skim off any excess fat that remains. In a saucepan bring the gravy to a final boil and then correct the seasoning. Serve the gravy in a sauceboat. (Serves 6).

Sauté de Lapin au Moutard à la Curnonsky
Sautéed Rabbit with Mustard Sauce à la Curnonsky

1 rabbit, about 2½ lb (about 1 kilo)	½ lb (225 gr) lean thickly sliced bacon, diced
1½ lb potatoes, peeled and quartered	2 Tbsp vegetable oil
2 Tbsp butter, softened	2 tsp mustard seeds
2 Tbsp sweet cream mixed with 1 Tbsp milk	1 tsp dried thyme
	½ cup white wine
salt and pepper to taste	¾ cup sweet cream
	1 Tbsp Dijon mustard

Place the potatoes in a pot, pour over cold water to cover, bring to a boil and cook until soft through (about 25 minutes). Force the potatoes through a strainer into a heavy saucepan to form a mash. Then cook briefly over a moderate heat until the potatoes begin to stick to the bottom. At this point beat in the butter, the sweet cream and milk mixture, and salt and pepper to taste. Set aside to keep warm.

Place the bacon in a saucepan, pour over cold water, bring to a boil and then simmer for 10 minutes. Drain and pat the bacon dry.

Cut the rabbit into pieces (leaving the thighs whole). Heat the oil in a heavy skillet until hot but not smoking and in this brown the rabbit pieces, turning once (about 5 minutes on each side). Drain the oil from the pan, add the bacon and brown lightly for about 1 minute. Add the mustard seeds and thyme. Add the wine and bring to a boil, scraping the bottom and sides of the pan with a spatula. Add the sweet cream and then cook over a high heat until the cream is reduced to about half of its volume (5–7 minutes). Reduce the heat to very low, remove the rabbit pieces to a warm plate, and swirl the Dijon mustard into the sauce.

Warm four plates, on each plate place a scoop of mashed potatoes, pour a small amount of sauce on each plate and place several rabbit pieces on top of the sauce. Serve immediately. (Serves 4).

Marcel Rouff, 1877–1936

The Melting Pot

The Napoleon of gourmets and the Beethoven of cooking are only two of the superlatives bestowed upon Monsieur Dodin-Bouffant, a retired magistrate who lived in the 1830s in a small town in the Jura, a French region near the Swiss border, and devoted his life to the art of French cuisine. Dodin-Bouffant is the protagonist of *La Vie et la Passion de Dodin-Bouffant, Gourmet*, a novel by Marcel Rouff published in 1920 that has since become a classic among epicureans. Rouff, who was born in Geneva but lived in France, wrote several novels and biographies but is remembered mostly for his collaboration with restaurant critic Curnonsky on a series of guides to the regional food of France.

Dodin-Bouffant and his friends enjoyed *amuse-gueules* such as mushroom and shrimp jellies, preserved trout stuffed with tarragon and chopped olives, tubs of roe pickled with cloves, and iced eels stuffed with pounded prawns. These were some of the delights made by Dodin's cook, who also served "an uninterrupted dream of veal-birds with scented stuffings" along with legs of mutton, fricassees, and sheep's tongues *en papillotes*, among other dishes. In the most celebrated scene of the book, Dodin-Bouffant, after having dined at the table of the Crown Prince of Eurasia, enjoying a dinner involving sixty dishes, reciprocates by

offering the
prince a modest
meal featuring only *pot-au-feu*, the dish
so well beloved by the French. The Prince, who is at first offended by
such a coarse dish, soon marvels at the charms of the *pot-au-feu*: "The
beef itself, lightly rubbed with saltpeter and then gone over with salt,
was carved into slices of a flesh so fine that its mouth-melting texture
could actually be seen. The aroma it gave forth was not only that of
beef-juice smoking like incense, but the energetic smell of tarragon with
which it was impregnated and the few, very few, cubes of transparent,
immaculate bacon in the larding."

Dodin-Bouffant was probably modeled after the great gastronome Brillat-Savarin, to whom Rouff dedicated the book and whose

guide *Physiologie du Goût* is mentioned in the novel. James de Coquet, who wrote the introduction to the 1970 French edition, knew Rouff during his last years and describes him as "a refined man, courteous, delicate, erudite, of whom one might say that he was the opposite of a gourmand," but judging by the discriminating methods by which Dodin-Bouffant selected his guests, one can speculate that his creator had stronger passions. Most of Dodin-Bouffant's guests did not pass his scrutinizing tests. One guest failed to recognize in the cream of a cauliflower sauce "the exotic caress of a pinch of nutmeg", another mistook a superb Châteauneuf-du-Pape for Beaujolais, and a third could not tell the difference between beef from Nivernais and beef from Franche-Comté. Others were scorned for ignoring the superfluous salt in a purée of cardoons.

Pot-au-Feu

1½ lb (675 gr) beef marrow bones, cut into 2″ lengths
4 leeks, white and green parts separated, trimmed and washed
2 lb (900 gr) short ribs of beef
2 lb (900 gr) boned beef shank
Brittany sea salt or kosher salt as required
3 medium onions, each studded with 1 clove

1 bouquet garni made by tying together 12 sprigs parsley, 8 whole peppercorns, ½ tsp fresh thyme, ¼ tsp fennel seeds, 1 bay leaf in a cheesecloth
1 cabbage, about 1¼ lb (575 gr)
6 carrots, peeled
1 small celery root, peeled and cubed

Wrap each of the marrow bones in a green leaf of the leek and tie with kitchen string.

Using kitchen string, tie the beef ribs and beef shank in two separate bundles. Place these in a large kettle and pour over cold water to cover. Over a medium-high flame bring the water to a simmer, taking care not to let it boil. Let the meat simmer for about 10 minutes and then skim the stock very carefully. Continue cooking for 30 minutes longer, repeat the skimming process several times until the liquids are clear.

To the kettle add the coarse salt, onions, bouquet garni and remaining green portions of the leeks. Skim again and simmer gently, skimming often, for about 2 hours longer.

About ½ hour before serving add the marrow bones, submerging them completely in the liquids.

Place the cabbage in a pot, pour over water, cover, bring to a boil and cook until tender (about 15 minutes). At the same time put the white portions of the leeks, the carrots and the celery root into another pot and cook these in the same way until tender (about 40 minutes). Drain the vegetables, transfer them to a large serving platter and keep warm in the oven.

Remove the beef from the kettle, cut off the kitchen string binding the bundles, cut into slices or chunks and place these on the platter with the vegetables. Discard the onions, bouquet garni and green portions of the leek. Remove and discard the leek wrappers from the marrow bones and place the bones on the platter alongside the meat. Arrange the cooked vegetables on the platter, ladle several Tbsp of the vegetable broth over the dish and serve at once. Ideally serve with coarse salt, Dijon mustard and *cornichons*. (Serves 8–10).

Alice B. Toklas, 1877–1967

To Please Gertrude

Alice B. Toklas was far from the best cook in Paris, but she certainly fed the most interesting members of the literary and artistic circles of her day, among them Thornton Wilder, Pablo Picasso, and Ernest Hemingway. Toklas always liked eating, but until she began living with Gertrude Stein in 1908, she had little interest in cooking. It was only when Stein informed her that the servants would be out on Sunday nights that Toklas was more or less forced to step into the kitchen.

The first dishes she produced were the simple California dishes she knew, but as she became more confident her repertoire expanded. On one occasion, when "Gertrude could not decided whether she preferred turkey stuffed with mushrooms, chestnuts or oysters", she simply included all three. On another occasion, when Picasso came to lunch, she prepared sea bass according to a somewhat odd theory she had learned from her grandmother, who felt that once a fish had been caught, it should have no further contact with water. Toklas poached the fish in wine and butter, covered it with red mayonnaise and topped it with sieved hard-boiled eggs, truffles and finely chopped *fines herbs*. When she served it to Picasso, he remarked that it would have been more appropriate for Matisse.

In 1952, Harper's commissioned Toklas to write a cookbook that was to include recipes and tales of her life with Stein, who had died in 1946. As she had a pressing deadline and not enough recipes, Toklas asked friends to help out. One of them, the artist Brion Gysin, gave her a recipe for hashish fudge. When the book was published in the United States in the same year, the publisher omitted the recipe, observing that "it will not sit very well with the members of the Baptist Church in the State of Iowa." In the UK this recipe was included in *The Alice B. Toklas Cookbook* and created a small scandal.

Toklas' recipes were often as eccentric as her appearance, and one can envision her in the kitchen, wearing her ill fitting dresses, high lace-

up shoes and hats decorated with enormous feathers. Thornton Wilder and Hemingway found her cooking delightful, but Zelda Fitzgerald, who quickly joined the list of people banned from Stein's salon, wrote that it was "incredibly bad."

When Toklas and Stein visited Seville in 1922, they dined at the El Burladero restaurant, where the chef concluded that Stein was "a silly little lady who took herself far too seriously" but was enchanted with Toklas, to whom he dedicated a dish. Even though the dish is known throughout the rest of Spain as "ducklings and olives in sherry" at the El Burladero it is still listed on the menu as *Patito Alice B. Toklas*.

Patito Alice B. Toklas
Duckling Alice B. Toklas

1 duckling, about 4½ lb (2 kilos)
2–3 slices onion
2 cloves garlic, whole
½ cup dry white wine
¾ cup green olives, pitted and chopped coarsely
2 Tbsp olive oil
1 medium onion, chopped coarsely

3 cloves garlic, chopped finely
½ cup chicken stock
½ cup dry Sherry
2 carrots, sliced thinly
1 bouquet garni made by tying together four sprigs of parsley and two bay leaves
6 whole peppercorns
salt to taste

Place the onion slices and whole garlic cloves in the cavity of the duckling. Tie the bird and prick all over with the tines of a fork. Place the duckling in a lightly greased roasting pan and roast in a medium oven for 1 hour, again pricking the duck after 30 minutes. Transfer the duckling to a preheated platter and cut into convenient serving pieces. Set aside to keep warm.

With a spoon remove the excess fat from the pan. Add ¼ cup of dry white wine to the pan and heat over a low flame, scraping the sides and bottom with a wooden spoon. Set aside for later use.

Place the olives and remaining dry white wine in a small saucepan, bring to the boil and then boil gently for 5 minutes. Drain the olives.

In a shallow flameproof casserole dish heat the olive oil and in this sauté together the chopped onion and chopped garlic until the onion is translucent. Add the stock, sherry, carrots, bouquet garni, peppercorns and the liquids earlier set aside. Simmer for 5 minutes. Add the duck to the casserole. Stir gently, cover and bake for 45 minutes longer in an oven that has been preheated to low. At the end of cooking, transfer the duck pieces to a preheated serving platter. Strain the sauce into a small saucepan, pressing with the back of a spoon to extract all of the liquids. Add 2 Tbsp of water to the casserole dish, heat gently, scraping the sides and bottom with a wood spoon and then add these liquids to the sauce. Stir in the drained olives, heat and pour over the duck. Serve hot. (Serves 4–6).

James Joyce, 1882–1941

Continental Fare

J ames Joyce is known to have spent remarkable sums of money on food. A native of Dublin, Joyce left Ireland with his would-be wife, Nora Barnacle, in 1904, and settled in Trieste on the Adriatic Sea. He later moved to Paris, where he lived from 1920 until 1941.

While there, he spent so much time in restaurants that some considered him a gourmet, but Sylvia Beach, the owner of Shakespeare & Company, a book shop that served tea and coffee and was then a haven for expatriate writers in Paris, and who published Joyce's masterpiece *Ulysses* in 1922, was probably right when she said that Joyce was interested in fine food only as long as it had something to do with his work. "He urged his family and the friends who might be dining with him to choose the best food on the menu...he himself ate scarcely anything," Beach commented. Art historian Louis Gillet observed that Joyce "always toyed with his food as if searching for something, and would then push back his plate with a disgusted look."

Joyce's favorite restaurant in Paris was Fouquet's on the Champs-Elysées, but he also spent considerable time in the cafés of Montparnasse, among them Les Deux Magots and Closerie des Lilas where he

sat with Hemingway and Ezra Pound, and of course at Shakespeare & Company, which had become a second home for him.

There are many references to food in Joyce's work, as for example the famous dinner in "The Dead", but the most celebrated scene is in one chapter of *Ulysses*, "Lestrygonians", an episode echoing Odysseus' encounter with the cannibals, which is devoted almost entirely to food. In this chapter, Bloom is looking for a restaurant at which to have his lunch. His search takes him on a long voyage along the streets of Dublin, where he observes Mrs. Breen with "flakes of pastry on the gusset of her dress," and sees Theodore Purefoy, the Methodist, who eats "saffron buns and milk and soda lunch in the educational dairy."

He wanders in to join the customers in the restaurant of the Burton Hotel, but the sight of the beastly men perched "on high stools by the bar, hats shoved back, at the tables calling for more bread no charge, swilling, wolfing gobfuls of sloppy food, their eyes bulging," repulses him and in the end he opts for typical Continental fare, a Gorgonzola sandwich with a glass of Burgundy wine in Davy Byrne's pub.

The Burton restaurant is no longer there, but Davy Byrne's pub on Duke Street is still open. Bloom's favorite dish is mutton kidneys with a tang of "faintly scented urine", but this is not replicated on June 16, Bloomsday, the day the Irish celebrate *Ulysses*. Instead varieties of sausage are the popular fare there, including blood sausages, the drisheens that Daedalus orders for breakfast in *A Portrait of the Artist as a Young Man*.

Stuffed Mutton Kidneys

3 mutton kidneys, about ¾ lb
   (375 gr) each, trimmed and
   with the fat reserved
¾ lb (375 gr) bacon, in one
   piece
½ lb (225 gr) baby onions
¾ lb green peas, ideally fresh
8 cloves garlic, peeled
1 Tbsp Calvados or other apple
   brandy

1¼ cup apple cider
1 small bouquet garni made by
   tying together two sprigs
   each of parsley and thyme
   and a bay leaf
¼ cup butter, cut into small
   cubes
salt and pepper to taste

Trim and remove the membranes of the kidneys. With a sharp knife, finely dice the fat of the kidneys and then halve the kidneys lengthwise, cutting out the central white cores with the point of a knife. Cut the kidneys into 1¼″ (3 cm) cubes.

Place the bacon in a saucepan and pour over cold water to cover. Bring to the boil and let boil for 10 minutes. Drain and rinse under cold water. Cut off the rind with a knife and then cut the bacon into long thin slices.

Peel, wash and dry the onions and set aside. If using fresh peas, remove them from their shells, cover with water and bring to a boil. Let simmer gently for 3 minutes. Drain, rinse under cold water and set aside. If using frozen peas, simply defrost them and have them ready for use when required.

Put 3 Tbsp of the kidney fat in a large skillet and set over a very high flame, stirring with a spatula. Lightly season the kidneys and when the fat is very hot, throw them into the pan and cook quickly, stirring constantly for 1–2 minutes. Reduce the heat and cook the kidneys for another 3–4 minutes, so that they are still pink. Drain the kidneys and set aside.

In the same skillet in which the kidneys were cooked, heat the rest of the kidney fat. Add the bacon slices and brown them lightly, and then add the onions and unpeeled garlic. Sprinkle with the Calvados, add the cider and put in the bouquet garni. Cover the pan and simmer for 8 minutes. Add the peas and cook for 2–3 minutes longer. Remove the skillet from the heat and beat in the butter a little at a time. Discard the bouquet garni, season to taste with salt and pepper, add the kidneys and return to a very low heat, warming the kidneys in the sauce for 2–3 minutes. Serve hot. (Serves 4).

Drisheens
Irish Blood Sausages

about 3′ (1 meter) of sausage
  casings
2 Tbsp lard
¾ cup finely chopped onions
⅓ cup whipping cream
¼ cup breadcrumbs
2 beaten eggs
¼ teaspoon dried thyme

½ bay leaf, pulverized
1 teaspoon salt
¼ tsp ground mace
¼ tsp coriander
freshly ground pepper to taste
½ lb leaf lard diced into ½-inch
  cubes
2 cups fresh pork blood

In a skillet, melt the regular lard and in this sauté the chopped onions just until translucent. Remove from the flame and let cool for 15 minutes. Then, in a mixing bowl, combine with the whipping cream, breadcrumbs, eggs, thyme, bay leaf, salt, mace, coriander and pepper. Add the leaf lard and pork blood, mix well, and with this mixture fill the sausage casings. Fill the casings only about ¾ because the mixture will expand during the cooking process. Seal the casings by tying with kitchen string.

Place the filled casings in a large wire basket, taking care not to pack them too tightly. Bring water to a boil in a large pot, remove from the flame and plunge the basket into the water, making sure there is enough water to cover the sausages generously. Return to a low flame for about 15 minutes. During the cooking process if any of the sausages float to the surface of the water, prick with a toothpick to release the air. Test the sausages for doneness by piercing with the tines of a fork. If blood comes out continue to cook for about 5 minutes longer (when done the sausages should be barely firm).

Remove the sausages from the water and let cool. The sausages may be stored, refrigerated, for 3–5 days. To prepare for serving fry the sausages very gently in a heavy skillet until heated through. Ideal served with generously buttered mashed potatoes. (Serves 4).

Suzette, late-19th century

The Mysterious Dame

There may be no dish that better demonstrates the sense of mystery and charm that surrounds the naming of French culinary inventions than the world famous Crêpes Suzette.

The most popular tale has it that Henri Charpentier, a fifteen-year-old assistant waiter at Monte Carlo's Café de Paris, came out with the dish in 1895, when he was serving crêpes for the Prince of Wales, the future King Edward VII of England. The crêpes were precooked in the kitchen, but were heated in a chaffing dish with liqueurs in front of the guests. Charpentier, who later became a world famous chef, wrote in his memoirs: "It was quite by accident as I worked in front of a chaffing dish that the cordials caught fire...I tasted it. It was, I thought, the most delicious melody of sweet flavors I had ever tasted..." He wanted to call the dish Crêpes Princesse, but the Prince asked that the dish be named after a young lady present at the meal, apparently a daughter of one of his friends. And so Crêpes Suzette was born, a dessert that, as Charpentier put it, "would reform a cannibal into a civilized gentleman."

There are, however, alternate versions. One story has it that Suzette was not a young and innocent girl, but one of Edward's mistresses, and the dish was invented not in Monte Carlo but in the fashionable spa of Baden-Baden. Yet another tale has Suzette as a well known courtesan for whom Charpentier named the dish when he was head of the kitchen of a well-known Paris restaurant. A chef named Joseph Donon claimed that he invented the dish for a German actress, Suzanne Reichenberg, but others argued that Donon did nothing more than supply the daily allotment of pancakes for a theater production in the *Comedie Francaise*, in which a maid named Suzette was serving pancakes. It has also been claimed that crêpes Suzette was created by the chef Jean Reboux for King Louis x v, at the behest of Princess Suzette de Carignan, who wanted to win the King's heart.

Crêpes Suzette

FOR THE SAUCE:

1 tsp lemon rind, cut very thinly

1 tsp tangerine rind, cut very thinly (note: although purists may insist to the contrary, orange rind may be substituted)

1 tsp sugar

2 drops vanilla extract

½ cup butter

2 Tbsp each of kirsch and Grand Marnier liqueurs

FOR THE CRÊPES:

2½ cups flour, sifted
pinch of salt
4 whole eggs + 2 egg yolks
1¾ cups milk
1 Tbsp Curacao liqueur
2 drops vanilla extract

1 Tbsp butter, heated until
 light brown
¼ cup melted butter, for
 cooking
¼ cup sugar

In a jar combine the lemon and tangerine rinds with the sugar and vanilla extract. Let stand tightly covered, for at least 24 but not more than 48 hours.

Prepare the crêpes: Sift the flour into a large bowl and make a well in the center. Add the salt and then add, one at a time, the whole eggs and egg yolks, working the batter with a wood spoon until the mixture is well distributed. Add the milk, Curacao, vanilla, and browned butter and work together until the batter is completely smooth. Cover and let stand at room temperature for about 1½ hours.

Before cooking the crêpes, check the batter. It should have the consistency of light cream, just thick enough to coat a wooden spoon. To cook the crêpes, butter a 7″ crêpe pan or other low heavy skillet of the same size with some of the melted butter. Heat until a drop of batter dropped in the pan sizzles. In order to test the consistency of the batter and check the heat, make a first crêpe by pouring 2–3 Tbsp of the batter into the pan, turning the pan quickly so that the bottom is evenly coated, keeping in mind that the crêpes should be extremely thin. Cook over a medium flame until the crêpe is browned on the bottom and, with a metal spatula, turn and brown the second side. If the batter is overly thick, thin the mixture by adding milk a teaspoonful at a time.

Proceed to make the remaining crêpes, adding butter to the pan only if the crêpes begin to stick. If the crêpes are to be used immediately they may be piled one on top of the other. If they are to be stored, separate each layer with waxed paper, cover and refrigerate until ready for use. Just before final preparation, fold each crêpe so that it forms a triangular shape.

Make the sauce: In a heavy skillet melt the butter and, when it begins to bubble add half each of the kirsch and Grand Marnier. When the mixture is warm carefully flame the liqueurs. As the flame dies down add the lemon and tangerine mixture. Bring the sauce to the boil and into this place the crêpes, turning once.

Transfer the crepes to a pre-warmed serving plate. In a small attractive saucepan gently heat the remaining liqueurs. Bring the crêpes and the liqueurs to the table, pour the liqueurs over the crêpes and flame again. Serve while flaming. (Serves 4–6).

Jules Maigret, 1884–c. 1980
The Inspector's *Plat du Jour*

In all of France, no policeman ever ate better than Jules Maigret, writer Georges Simenon's laconic Chief Inspector of Paris' Police Judiciaire. As a detective who spent most of his life pursuing murderers, he often found himself in a host of places and situations where the most logical thing to do was to accept whatever food or drink was being offered. Indeed, the cafés and bistros of Paris, as well as those in the provinces, offered him an abundance of good solid dishes.

One can visualize Maigret sitting in a small bistro, eating soup or perhaps potage or satisfying his appetite with *andouillettes* (pork sausages similar to chitterlings). On a cold rainy day he might order *choucroute garni*, and then, as time passes while he perhaps waits to see if the suspect under surveillance is leaving the apartment building across the street, or waits for a phone call from Inspector Lucas, he will enjoy a glass of *marc*, a brandy distilled from grape or apple residue and adored by the French. Maybe, if he succeeds in solving the affair at hand, he will indulge in a small snifter of Armagnac.

During Maigret's very first case, described in the novel *Pietr-le-Leton*, he was forced to seek shelter in the Le Vieux Calvados on an early morning stakeout. Le Vieux Calvados was a café housed in a long, narrow building, with a single step that led down to a cool room where "reflections gleamed here and there on the tin covered counter and where the bottles appeared to have been set in place for ages." Charmed by the setting, the detective was pleased when the proprietor suggested a few slices of sausage in wine sauce and a glass of Cognac for breakfast.

As it was a long stakeout, Maigret was in the café for quite some time. At first he was taken aback when the patron insisted that he join him every half hour for a glass of Calvados, but after a while he settled

comfortably into the pattern, realizing that "this was a ritual, a kind of craze with the owner." He also understood that it was this ritual that accounted for the owner's "blotched complexion and for the wateriness in which his eyes were constantly swimming."

Of course, some cases and some days provided better culinary fare than others. When Maigret was sent to the town of Luçon as temporary regional superintendent, for example, for his first day's lunch he was regaled with a marvelous shrimp mousse which was followed by an exquisite beef tongue in raisin sauce.

When last heard of, Maigret was retired and living quietly in Meung-sur-Loire, a small town near Orleans boasting a twelfth century church and a chateau. He was dining primarily on the good country-style cuisine of Madame Maigret, including her excellent *coq-au-vin* with just a drop of sloe gin, and he was, of course, continuing to enjoy the preserves his sister-in-law sent from Clermont-Ferrand. Despite the warnings of his doctor, he was still making his way into the village at least once a day, there to sip two or more glasses of dry white wine.

Saucisse au Vin Blanc
Sausages in White Wine

1 lb (450 gr) firm sausages
   (e.g. knockwurst), sliced ½″
   (1 cm) thick
6 Tbsp dry white wine

2 pimentos cut in strips
2 Tbsp parsley, chopped
3–4 cloves garlic, minced

In a large heavy skillet sauté the sausages until lightly browned.

Pour off most of the fat, pour in the wine and using a wooden spoon scrape the pan well over a low flame. Add the remaining ingredients and transfer the mixture to a small earthenware casserole dish. Bake in a medium oven for 15 minutes. Serve hot. (Serves 4 for breakfast or 2 for lunch).

Mousse aux Crevettes
Shrimp Mousse

1 bouquet garni, made by tying
   together 3 sprigs parsley, 2
   sprigs thyme and 1 bay leaf
1 onion, peeled but whole
1 lb (450 gr) shrimps
1 Tbsp gelatin
½ cup each apple and celery,
   both minced

salt and paprika to taste
dash of Tabasco
1 cup mayonnaise
¼ cup lemon juice
1 tsp dry mustard
½ cup sweet cream
cucumber slices for garnish

In a saucepan bring a large amount of lightly salted water to a boil. Add the bouquet garni and onion and return to the boil. Add the shrimps and boil gently just until the shrimps turn pink (3–4 minutes). Let the shrimps cool and then peel and de-vein the shrimps. Chop them coarsely.

Dissolve the gelatin in ½ cup of boiling water.

In a mixing bowl, combine the celery, apple, shrimps, salt, paprika and Tabasco. In a smaller bowl combine the mayonnaise, lemon juice and dry mustard and into this pour the gelatin mixture, mixing well.

Whip the cream until stiff and then fold into the mayonnaise dressing. Fold this into the shrimp mixture and stir together gently but thoroughly. Transfer to a 23 cm ring mold which has been pre-dampened. Chill thoroughly and served cold on a well-chilled serving plate. Garnish with thin cucumber slices. (Serves 6).

Langue de Bœuf à la Lyonnaise
Beef Tongue in Raisin Sauce

1 fresh beef tongue, about 2¼ lb (1 kilo)	½ cup blanched almonds
2 large onions, halved	3 Tbsp flour
2 medium carrots, halved lengthwise	1 cup seedless raisins
4 ribs celery, with leaves	¼ cup crushed ginger snap cookies
6 sprigs parsley	1 tsp lemon rind, grated
8 whole peppercorns	salt and pepper to taste

Place the tongue in a large kettle and add the onions, carrots, celery, parsley and peppercorns. Cover with boiling water and simmer, uncovered, until the tongue is tender (about 3 hours), skimming the foam from the surface of the liquid periodically. Remove the tongue and run under cold water for several minutes. Under running water peel the tongue and trim off the fat, reserving 6 Tbsp of the fat. Reserve the stock in which the tongue was cooked, and when cooled skim the foam from the surface.

Split the almonds and simmer them in a saucepan with 2 cups of water for 20 minutes. Add the raisins and simmer ½ hour longer. Strain the sauce, reserving the liquids and solids separately.

In a heavy skillet melt the reserved fat and to this add the flour slowly, stirring until blended. Gradually add the raisins and almonds, the almond liquid and enough of the reserved stock to make 3½ cups in all. To this add the crushed ginger snaps and lemon rind. Correct the seasoning with salt and pepper to taste. Pour part of the sauce over the tongue and serve the remainder in a sauceboat. (Serves 4–6).

Caesar Cardini, 1896–1956
Salad Days

Few dishes better illustrate the convoluted history of the culinary world than Caesar Salad. Some trace the dish to Giacomo Junia, an Italian cook in Chicago who allegedly named it after Julius Caesar circa 1903. Others speculate that it was created by the great chef Georges Auguste Escoffier and named after his partner César Ritz. Most food historians, however, are in agreement that the dish was created by Caesar Cardini, an Italian immigrant to the United States.

During the period of Prohibition, Caesar Cardini and his brother Alex owned a hotel and restaurant in Tijuana, Mexico, just across the border from San Diego, where they resided. According to Rosa, Caesar's daughter, the dish was first made on the fourth of July 1924, when the town was so crowded with intoxicated Americans that the restaurant had begun to run short of food. Caesar is said to have tossed together a salad from whatever was left in the kitchen, the original recipe including romaine lettuce, coddled eggs, croutons, grated Parmesan cheese, Worcestershire sauce, crushed garlic, olive oil, lemon juice, salt and pepper. The salad dressing was made at tableside, and the dressing was spooned ceremoniously over the lettuce leaves that were placed stem side out, in a circle, and served on a flat plate so that it could be eaten with the fingers.

The salad became so popular that many claimed credit for it, among them, Alex Cardini, Caesar's brother and partner, whose version also contained anchovies; Paul Maggiora, a partner of the Cardinis and a veteran of the Italian air force, who called it Aviators' Salad; and Livio Santini, a worker at the restaurant, who claimed he got the recipe from his mother.

It became fashionable among the Hollywood crowd to drive to Tijuana for a Caesar Salad, and it is said that Clark Gable, Jean Harlow, and W.C. Fields were regular guests there. Julia Child visited the place with her parents when she was nine years old, and later wrote about the tableside ceremony in her book *From Julia Child's Kitchen*. Wallis Simpson, the future wife of Edward VIII, a frequent guest at the Caesar's Palace Hotel in Tijuana, is alleged to have introduced the Caesar salad to European chefs, and was the first to cut the lettuce leaves into bite-sized pieces to avoid having to eat it with the fingers.

Following the repeal of Prohibition, the Cardinis sold the restaurant and moved to Los Angeles, and in 1948 patented the salad dressing, which is still packaged and sold as Cardini's Original Caesar Dressing Mix.

In 1953, Caesar Salad was voted the "greatest recipe to originate from the Americas in fifty years" by the International Society of Epicures in Paris. Today many chefs supplement the original recipe with chicken, shrimp or lobster.

Caesar Salad

1 large head romaine lettuce, trimmed
1 cup olive oil
3 cups French bread, with crusts intact, cut into ½" (1 cm) cubes
2 large cloves garlic, peeled
8 anchovy fillets
1 tsp Worcestershire sauce

1 tsp dry mustard
2 Tbsp lemon juice
1 tsp each salt and freshly ground black pepper
2 egg yolks from large eggs, at room temperature
½ cup Parmesan cheese, grated
¼ cup Parmesan cheese, shaved

Cut the lettuce leaves into 1½" (4 cm) pieces, wash and drain these well, pat dry and refrigerate for ½ hour to make the leaves crisp.

In a skillet heat ½ cup of the olive oil and in this fry the bread cubes until crisp and golden. Drain on paper toweling and set aside.

Place the garlic cloves in a large wooden salad bowl. With a wooden spoon, mash the cloves against the bowl, coating the bowl well. Remove most of the mashed garlic from the bowl. Add the anchovy fillets and rub these around the entire bowl but in this case leave the anchovy pieces in the bowl.

Add the mustard, Worcestershire sauce, lemon juice, black pepper, and egg yolks and blend well. Slowly drizzle in the remaining olive oil, mixing with a wire whisk until a creamy mayonnaise type dressing forms. Add the lettuce, croutons, grated Parmesan cheese and salt. Toss well, sprinkle over the shaved Parmesan cheese and serve from the salad bowl. (Serves 4).

Ernest Hemingway, 1899–1961

Café Days

During his days in Paris, Ernest Hemingway liked to think of himself as a person in command of his appetites. "Hunger," he said, "is a good discipline and you learn many things from it." He also wrote that people can "handle themselves better" when they cut down on food, for eating a lot inhibited what he called "hunger-thinking." Despite a good deal of intellectualization, hunger was an experience to which Hemingway rarely treated himself. The son of a wealthy physician, he spent his youth in a comfortable suburb of Chicago, and when he moved to Paris in 1921, the inheritance of his wife, Hadley, allowed him to afford frequent visits to numerous bars and restaurants.

In the seven years he lived in Paris, Hemingway made it a habit to do his writing in cafés. He used to visit various cafés during the daytime hours, when customers were more scarce, sitting alone with his notebooks and pencils. He was especially fond of La Closerie des Lilas, which he considered one of the best cafés in Paris. Describing his attraction to the café, he wrote: "It was warm inside in the winter, and in the spring and fall it was very fine outside when the tables were set under the shade of the trees." He also enjoyed the Closerie because it was only a short stroll from his rooms on the rue Notre-Dame-des-Champs and

because most of the literary expatriates of the day sat at other cafés, this leaving him the quiet to write.

It was there, on one of the marble tabletops, that he wrote his novel *The Sun Also Rises*. One of his favorite dishes at the Closerie was "a simple masterpiece of little radishes and sautéed goose liver with mashed potatoes." He was also fond of oysters, and in his memoir of his years in Paris, *A Moveable Feast*, he elaborates on this subject: "As I ate the oysters with their strong taste of the sea and their faint metallic taste that the cold white wine washed away, leaving only the sea taste and the succulent texture, and as I drank their cold liquid from each shell and washed it down with the crisp taste of the wine, I lost the empty feeling and began to be happy, and to make plans."

Another of Hemingway's favorite places was Brasserie Lipp. There he enjoyed sitting on one of the banquettes, his back against the mirrored wall. He would start with a beer and then follow with an order of potatoes in oil and mustard sauce. "The beer was very cold and wonderful to drink," he wrote in *A Moveable Feast*, "the *pommes a l'huile* were firm and marinated and the olive oil was delicious. I ground black pepper over the potatoes and moistened the bread in the oil. After the first heavy draught of beer I drank and ate very slowly. When the *pommes a l'huile* were gone I ordered another serving of *cervelas*. This was a sausage like a heavy, wide frankfurter split in two and covered with mustard sauce. I mopped up all of the oil and all of the sauce with bread and drank the beer slowly until it began to lose its coldness and then I finished it and ordered a *demi* and watched it drawn."

Pommes de Terre a l'Huile
Potatoes in Oil and Mustard Sauce

3 Tbsp olive oil

2 Tbsp each white wine, beef stock and white wine vinegar

1 Tbsp sugar

2 cloves garlic, chopped finely

6 spring onions, whites only, diced

1 tsp powdered mustard

4 medium potatoes

1 Tbsp parsley, chopped, for garnish

salt and pepper to taste

baguette for serving

12 small radishes for serving

2 or 4 *cervelas* or knockwurst sausages, cooked and split in half lengthwise for serving (optional)

Dijon mustard to accompany the sausage

In a small mixing bowl combine the oil, vinegar, sugar, garlic, spring onions, mustard, white wine, salt and pepper. Whip, and then cover and let stand at room temperature for 1–2 hours.

Bring lightly salted water to the boil in a large saucepan and then add the potatoes. Cook them until done but still firm. Remove from the water and peel. Allow the potatoes to cool until lukewarm and cut into ½″ (1 cm) slices. Pour over the dressing, toss lightly and let stand, covered, at room temperature, for about 1 hour. To serve, sprinkle over the parsley and serve with baguette, radishes and sausages. (Serves 4 as a first course or light lunch).

Sautéed Goose Liver

Hemingway's favorite dish at La Closerie des Lilas

1 goose liver, about 2½ lb
(1 kilo), with gall bladder
and veins removed and
soaked in cold water for 2
hours
1 Tbsp sugar
½ tsp ground ginger
½ tsp hot paprika
¼ cup goose or chicken fat, for
frying

3 Tbsp butter
1 or 2 apples, peeled and cut
into slices
1 or 2 onions, sliced and
separated into rings
2 Tbsp dry Sherry
mashed potatoes for serving
(recommended but
optional)

In a small glass combine the sugar, ginger and
paprika, mixing well. Dry the liver with a cloth
and sprinkle with the seasoning mixture.

In a heavy skillet melt the goose fat,
and sauté the liver until tender and done.

In a separate skillet melt the butter and
in this sauté the apples and onions together just
until the onions start to brown. Sprinkle over the
Sherry.

To serve, slice the liver, transfer the slices to a preheated serving
plate, and heap over the sautéed apples and onions. Ideal when served
with mashed potatoes. (Serves 6 as a first course).

Chicken Hemingway

The following dish was dedicated to Hemingway by a chef at The Terrace Inn in Petoskey, Michigan, where Hemingway occasionally stayed during fishing trips.

4 chicken breasts, skinned and
    boned
1 cup all purpose flour
1 tsp salt
2 tsp pepper
2–3 Tbsp olive oil
1 cup chicken stock

2 Tbsp fresh basil, chopped
¼ cup dry white wine
¼ cup sweet cream
3 Tbsp dried red cherries
fettuccini pasta, cooked, for
    serving

In a shallow bowl mix together the flour, salt and pepper and into this dip the chicken breasts, coating well.

In a skillet heat the olive oil and in this sauté the chicken breasts for 3 to 4 minutes on each side.

Add the chicken stock, basil, and wine. Simmer until the liquids are reduced by half. Add the sweet cream, simmer gently until slightly thickened, add the dried cherries and heat through. Serve over the pasta. (Serves 2).

A.J. Liebling, 1904–1963
An American in Paris

W hen he was twenty-two, A.J. Liebling spent a year at the Sorbonne, and even though he actually attended very few classes, he learned things that stood him in good stead for the rest of his life. The Paris he discovered was the same city with which Hemingway and Gertrude Stein fell in love. "Perhaps more than anything else," he later reminisced "it was in Paris that I learned to eat."

In 1935 Liebling joined the staff of the *New Yorker* magazine. Within a short time his "Wayward Press" columns had become models for fine journalistic writing. Whether he was writing about Rabelais, Hemingway or Mohammed Ali, his language was idiomatic, ringing with precision and rich in details. And in nearly everything he wrote, there was some reference to food.

Always surrounded by friends, Liebling was more a glutton than a gourmet. He once wrote, for example, of an unforgettable afternoon spent with his friend and mentor Yves Mirande, "one of the last great gastronomes of France." In a small restaurant on the rue Saint-Augustin, the two lunched on "raw Bayonne ham and fresh figs, a hot sausage baked in a pastry shell, several fillets of pike in a rich Nantua sauce, a leg of lamb with anchovy sauce, a half dozen artichokes served with goose liver and four kinds of cheese, all washed down with two good bottles of Bordeaux red and one of Champagne." To the amazement of everybody in the restaurant, as soon as they had finished their lunch, they immediately began to plan dinner.

On another occasion, at Chez Benoit, the pair started their dinner with a large trout served "with enough melted butter to raise the cholesterol count of an entire regiment of soldiers beyond belief." With the trout, they drank a bottle of white wine from Alsace. This was followed by lobster quenelles with shrimp sauce, roast beef smothered in steamed vegetables and a pair of quails in honey sauce served with fresh figs and asparagus. With the beef they had a bottle of Chateau Petrus and with the hens a bottle of Cheval Blanc. They followed lunch with three bottles of Krug Champagne, drinking toasts to their lovers, their countries and the owner of the restaurant.

The restaurant on rue Saint-Augustin no longer exists, but many of Liebling's favorite eating spots are still open for business. Chez Benoit is still to be found at 20 rue Saint-Martin; Drouant still exists on the place Gaillon; the Closerie de Lilas is still to be found at 171 blvd du Montparnasse, and Laperouse, at 51 quai des Grands-Augustins, continues to delight its regular clients. That most of these places have not even a single star in the Michelin guide would please Liebling, for he held the book in a particular disdain.

Quennelles d'Homard au Sauce de Crevettes
Lobster Quenelles in Shrimp Sauce

FOR THE QUENELLES:

1½ lb (675 gr) lobster meat
(can also use trout or pike)

3 cups whipping cream, well
chilled

2 egg whites, beaten

grated nutmeg to taste

salt and white pepper to taste

dash or two of Cognac and
Tabasco

FOR THE SAUCE:

1 lb (450 gr) shrimps, in their
shells

2½ cups milk

1 cup chicken stock

½ small onion, chopped finely

¼ cup sweet cream

2 Tbsp pastis liqueur (Pernod
or ouzo)

2 Tbsp butter

1½ Tbsp flour

4 tsp brandy

1 tsp tomato puree

1 clove garlic, minced

salt and pepper to taste

Run the lobster meat through the finest blade of a food chopper three times. Place the ground lobster in a large bowl placed comfortably on a bowl of ice. Using a wooden spoon, work the lobster into a smooth paste, and then slowly work in the beaten egg whites and season to taste with the nutmeg, salt, pepper, Cognac and Tabasco. While still over the ice, slowly add the whipping cream, blending constantly.

To form the quenelles, have ready two moderately large spoons of equal size, a small bowl of hot water and a well buttered baking tin. Leave one spoon in the hot water and with the other lightly scoop out just enough of the quenelle mixture to fill the spoon. Take the second spoon out of the hot water and invert it over the first to shape the quenelle. Do not press the spoons together: merely shape the quenelles.

To make the sauce, melt the butter in a large skillet and in this sauté the onion and garlic until soft but not browned. Stir in the flour and continue to cook, stirring constantly, until simmering but not boiling. Add the milk, stock, shrimp and salt and pepper to taste.

Bring to a boil and immediately reduce the heat and let simmer for 5–6 minutes.

Remove the shrimp from the skillet and shell them. Keep the shrimp to one side. Crush the shells and add these, the pastis and the brandy to the sauce. Simmer for 10 minutes and then strain the sauce. Stir in the tomato puree and the cream and correct the seasoning.

Arrange the quenelles in a buttered baking dish and over them arrange the shrimp. Pour the sauce over, covering generously, and bake in a medium-hot oven until the sauce is lightly browned and the quenelles have risen slightly (10–12 minutes). Serve immediately. (Serves 4–6).

Cailles au Miel et Figues
Quails in Honey Sauce with Figs

12 small or medium quails
3 Tbsp butter
1 cup sweet white wine (ideally Sherry or Sauternes)
12 fresh figs
1–2 Tbsp honey

dried thyme to taste
lemon juice to taste
cornstarch as required
salt and pepper to taste

Sprinkle the birds inside and out with salt, pepper and thyme. In a heavy skillet heat the butter and then sauté the birds for a few minutes on each side. Transfer the birds to an oven that has been preheated to hot and let cook for about 15 minutes until the birds have taken on a light pink color. Transfer the birds to a preheated serving platter, cover and set aside to keep warm.

Pour off the excess fat from the skillet, add the wine and cook over a medium flame, stirring and scraping the bottom and sides of the skillet, for about 1 minute. Add the figs and cook for 5 minutes, stirring occasionally. Season the sauce to taste with salt, pepper, honey, thyme and lemon juice. If the sauce is too thin mix a bit of cornstarch in some cold water and add it, stirring well. Correct the seasoning if necessary.

Serve by placing the figs around the birds on the serving platter and then strain the sauce over the birds. Serve at once. (Serves 6).

Oven Temperatures

	Fahrenheit	Celsius
Low	330	170
Medium	350	180
Medium–Hot	375	190
Hot	400	200
Very Hot	450	235

Index of Recipes

About the Author

Daniel Rogov

Daniel Rogov is Israel's most influential and preeminent restaurant and wine critic. He writes weekly wine and restaurant columns in the respected newspaper *Haaretz* and is the author of the best-selling annual, *Rogov's Guide to Israeli Wines*. Rogov contributes regularly to two prestigious international wine books—Hugh Johnson's *Pocket Wine Book* and Tom Stevenson's *Wine Report*—and maintains a wine and food website, Rogov's Ramblings, which can be found at www.tobypress.com/rogov.

About the Illustrator

Yael Hershberg

Yael Hershberg brings a background in the fine arts and 25 years' experience to her illustrations. She studied graphics and painting at the Rhode Island School of Design, the Cooper Union, and the Maryland Institute College of Art. She attracted special attention in the late 1990s with *The Jerusalem Haggadah*, a post-modern classic of Judaica. She lives and works in Jerusalem with her husband and family.

The fonts used in this book are from the Garamond family

The Toby Press publishes fine writing,
available at bookstores everywhere. For more information,
please contact *The* Toby Press at www.tobypress.com

00409 0141